ISSA

THE
GREATEST STORY
NEVER TOLD

ISSA

A NOVEL

LOIS DRAKE

SNOW MOUNTAIN ▲ PRESS™

ISSA
The Greatest Story Never Told
by Lois Drake

For information, please contact:
Summit University Press, 63 Summit Way,
Gardiner, MT 59030-9314 USA
Tel: 1-800-245-5445 or 406-848-9500
Web site: www.SummitUniversityPress.com

Library of Congress Control Number: 2006938749
ISBN: 978-1-932890-05-1

Cover design by George Foster www.fostercovers.com
Book design by Lynn M. Wilbert
Maps by William Groetzinger
Page *ii* based on oil painting by J. Michael Spooner

SNOW MOUNTAIN PRESS™
Snow Mountain Press is an imprint of Summit University Press®.
Printed in the United States of America

13   12   11   10   09   5   4   3   2   1

CONTENTS

*"These books say your
Jesus was here."*

Tibetan Buddhist Librarian
Himis Monastery, Ladakh, 1939

AUTHOR'S NOTE

Issa: The Greatest Story Never Told is inspired by *The Lost Years of Jesus,* by Elizabeth Clare Prophet. Mrs. Prophet's groundbreaking book documents ancient Buddhist manuscripts discovered more than a century ago in Ladakh that tell the story of Jesus' journey to the East as a teenager and his travels through India, Nepal, and Tibet as both student and teacher.

The time period of Jesus' "lost years" also saw the rise of a people known as the Kushans, whose civilization reached its zenith in the second and third centuries A.D. My collaborator, Fred Peck, compiled much information on the Kushans, seeking to unravel the mystery of their origins in central Asia.

I have woven this work of fiction from these two themes. It is an exploration of the ancient wisdom that might have guided Jesus on his journey. But more importantly, it is an invitation to you to ponder the question: What would it have been like to meet the teenager who would become the saviour of the world?

THE KUSHAN EMPIRE
First Century A.D.

1

THE DARK NIGHT

Northwestern China, Taklamakan Desert,
four years after the birth of Jesus

PERCHED ON A ROCK OVERLOOK, THE TWO LEADERS PEERED
into the encampment below. They could make out only the
flickering red-amber glow from the guards' campfire. Sounds
carried better than light on this dark night. The men heard
the stamp and snort of a restless horse, followed by an answer
from another nearby. A warm breeze came up from the desert
floor and with it the pungent smell of the herd. Now and
then, the murmur of shuffling animals came along with the
wind. A dog barked as if telling the animals to stay silent.
A gruff voice quieted the dog, and there was stillness again.

Two dark shadows, gliding against the rock, continued
their descent. No moon would show tonight. From the movement of the stars, the two knew an hour had passed since they
started out from their hidden camp on the plateau high above.
The black bluffs rose up from the canyon floor and formed
a half-circle fortress.

As they noiselessly felt their way down, the two leaders drew closer to the northern side of the Hun encampment. The tents were barely visible in the darkness, but they recalled the arrangement of the camp. They stopped and waited on the cliff, only a stone's throw from the closest tent and its sleeping occupants.

It would soon be time to begin. The sun would rise shortly. The men sat on the ledge above the valley floor and read the stars. Their ancestors had taught them precision with the sky.

The pair sat still and steadied their breathing. The large hoods of their coarse, red-brown cloaks hid their faces. They closed their eyes. With their rhythmic breathing, the two blended deeper and deeper into the walls of the canyon. The taller one took out a long gold chain that hung from his neck. On the chain was a small gold medallion, which he allowed to rest in the palm of his hand. Even when he was not looking at it, the imprint burned brightly in his mind: a six-pointed star, with a three-part flame at its center. The Signet. His thumb passed back and forth over the symbol. He opened his eyes again and felt renewed confidence, determination, and focus. It was time.

In a breath, their feet landed on the sandy floor. The pair split and went in opposite directions. They knew that, at this moment, other hooded comrades were gliding silently in from different points on the downwind side of the camp.

Only seven in total, they were enough.

Quickly, quickly. It would not be long before the dogs—yes!—there was the first mastiff, and a second, with wild and ferocious growls that awakened the sleeping Huns. More dogs barked. The hooded figures were past the first tents and nearing the horses' tethers. The dogs charged. In perfect calm, one of the silhouettes raised a hand and spoke a single word in his native Kushan tongue: "Peace."

The lead dog paused a fraction of a second.

Phhhht. Phhhht. Tiny blow reeds came from the cloaks of the other raiders, who quickly blew their darts into the dogs. The mastiffs ambled and whimpered slightly before they fell in sleep.

Sharp knives cut through the tethers holding the horses. Three animals had been tied to each of the strong iron rings driven into the ground—thirty horses in all. The silent team selected from those they had freed and led some away.

Only six animals—two stallions and four mares, stolen by the Huns from the Kushan village—were big horses, taller than a man. The marauding Hun party would be greatly set back if the rest were scattered. The herd was already nervous, stamping and snorting.

Alerted by the dogs and the sounds of the frightened horses, the encampment suddenly came to life. Torches were lit, and there was a clatter of weapons being gathered. The guards shouted and drew arrows, straining to see in the dark amid the animals. Some horses reared and the herd turned anxiously from side to side, ready to bolt. Dozens of torch-carrying men kept them in place.

One of the seven crossed deftly to the biggest, blue-black stallion. Stolen by the Huns, it was now the chief's horse and was under its own guard. The person made a soft clucking noise and met the eyes of the stallion, which stood transfixed. Suddenly a torch glared. Then came the shout of a guard: "Aiii yaah!"

The knife cut through the tether, and then the cloaked figure crouched under the horse for protection. It was too late to prevent the pain of an arrow that burned into the raider's shoulder. Falling back slightly, the raider broke off the arrow's shaft near the head and remained under the horse as the guards approached.

A thought rang out loudly in the raider's mind: "Yes. It's time." Suddenly there was a mighty, piercing, shattering sound as the team, perfectly in unison with a great shout from deep within their beings, invoked the sacred, ancient Tokharian words "Appakke Nakte!"—meaning Father God. It was only a moment, but it was sufficient.

Twenty-four freed Hun horses charged wildly in every direction. Overwhelmed, the guards and soldiers strained to see the intruders while at the same time attempting to stop the bolting horses. Tents collapsed as the wild-eyed steeds panicked and reared against them. Galloping and shouting echoed in every direction. Through it, six horses led by seven hooded figures trotted into the dark, moving closer and closer to the canyon wall before they disappeared.

THE SEVEN AND THEIR CAPTIVE STEEDS REACHED THE canyon wall. Looking back into the darkness, they saw pinpricks of torches bouncing up and down behind them. Soon these would gather to follow their tracks, which for now were still obscured by the confusion and the blackness.

An owl hooted. "Zhu Li," observed the tallest man. He answered the call and the party moved along the canyon wall another 200 paces. The wounded person, smaller than the others, walked toward the front of the group.

They paused to look out across the canyon floor. The torches below had coalesced into one group. Clearly the party's tracks had been discovered and the pursuers, some mounted, shouted with exuberance since they knew the tracks would lead to the impasse of the canyon wall. The cries of the Huns echoed wildly off the massive stone cliff.

The team never wavered. They crossed a dry creek bed and the tall one responded once more to the cry of the owl.

Past a rock face, they made a sudden turn where they entered a narrow slot canyon, the contorted and sculpted work of water and wind over eons. Its walls reached up to the sky. Twisting far into the cliff face, the slot canyon was only

a few inches wider than the horses. The group walked up-
stream. The creek bed was dry now, but when water did run,
it ran in a fury. The horses became nervous. The small raider
clucked consolingly and the group continued up the narrow
canyon.

The shouts of the Huns became softer because the turns
of the slot canyon muffled them. The tracks, however, would
quickly lead the way. There was no time to spare. Their secret
place could not be discovered. The group knew, as the Ancient
Ones had taught them, that timing was critical.

Once more the owl hooted. The call was returned. They
looked at the sky and the tall man raised his hand. For many
days he had been performing a sacred ritual at the home of
the Kushans, seeking the will and protection of Appakke
Nakte.

He watched the sky. Calmly he sent his vocal entreaty
for deliverance, calling upon the God of his fathers.

In the inner, mystical temple of his heart, his awareness
of God expanded beyond the physical world to hear the
Father's assurance: "Fear not. I AM with you."

He felt an unspoken confirmation of God's will pulsate
through his body. From that point of contact with God, he
sent a great release of sound as he chanted in devotion the
holy name, Appakke Nakte—many times, strongly, with
authority, again and again—until they heard the rumbling.
"Our Father, I thank thee. Thy will be done. May all life

be blessed by your wisdom, power, and love."

The rumbling became incredibly loud. It was the approach of that desert anomaly: the flash flood. For several days, the water had poured through the higher elevations. Cascading down, ever down, it would hit the canyon as a raging torrent. The slot canyon was created by the same process repeated over millennia. The approaching wall of water would instantly obliterate anything in its path. The roar was deafening.

Torchlight and a Hun's shout came from around the last turn. They heard another holler. The tall leader reached high on the rock wall and felt the palm-size six-pointed star carved there. He leaned his weight against it. The wall gave in slightly, and the seven pushed hard to move the stone enough to enter. A torch and the smiling face of Zhu Li greeted them inside. "Come! Come!" he beamed.

Seven hooded figures and the horses they led quickly passed through. They leaned back against the rock, heaved it in place, and immediately heard the roar of water surge by. Small drips trickled at the side of the stone door. The group and their charges were safe. The tracks were gone.

The Huns were scattered by water and confusion. Proceeding forward was impossible. Others in the rear turned around and raced from the oncoming water, in an attempt to either climb a high embankment or reach the open expanse of the valley floor.

The Hun chief, with his second-in-command, scrambled up a rocky slope and watched in disbelief as the torrent cut them off from the Kushans. "Barbarians!" the chief seethed with contempt and rage. "They have escaped tonight, but we will drive them from the highlands and kill every last one. Their king will pay dearly for this."

The aide spat on the ground. He was furious and his eyes narrowed as he surveyed the chaos. "Someone must pay for this blunder *tonight*," he hissed.

"Shall it be you?" the chief sneered back angrily. "Do you question my leadership?" The swarthy leader eyed his aide suspiciously before turning back to the scene. "Return to camp and execute the guards who were on duty," he said, and then kicked his horse and rode toward the valley.

BEHIND THE STONE DOOR, ZHU LI LED THE BAND BY torchlight around the curve of a subterranean passage. The light of the torch created a gleam upon his blue cap and blue silk tunic. A long braid of black hair lay flat upon his back. He was the height of the smallest raider, almost like a spirit hurrying ahead of the group. His dark, almond-shaped eyes sparkled with the flicker of the torch. White leggings, which wrapped his calves up to his blue silk trousers, stood out in the torchlight.

Finally, after several hundred paces, the group saw the

tunnel open to a huge cavern of blackness. The only light in the center of the expanse was Zhu Li's campfire. Over it was an iron pot, decorated with ancient symbols and simmering with steam. Around the edges of the cavern, dried clumps of grass and wooden pails of water awaited the horses. Carved jade decanters rested on ornate boxes, with delicate jade teacups next to them. Richly lacquered chopsticks lay across empty bowls awaiting rice, vegetables, and other delicacies simmering in the pot. The wounded figure sank in exhaustion onto one of the thick mats rolled out near the fire.

The tall man at last threw back his hood. A crop of red hair, cut straight across his forehead, and a beard trimmed close around his chin framed his blue eyes and ruddy complexion. Taktu's long, thin nose and high, angular cheekbones were a dramatic contrast to the flat nose and long face of Zhu Li, whose own beard hung daintily from his chin.

"Well done!" Taktu said to Zhu Li with a smile. Then, his brow furrowed and his voice turned low and serious as he said, "The queen is injured."

While the others tended to the horses, Taktu and Zhu Li bent down next to the small figure on the mat. King Taktu was the ruler of the Kushan people; generations before, the Huns had driven the Kushan out of the Tarim Basin, over the mountains, and into Bactria.

Taktu pushed back the hood from his wife's face. She lay with her eyes closed. She breathed deeply, with all her attention fixed on her breath, but her meditation was not enough to erase the pain and exhaustion showing on her face. Like her husband and the others in this elite, secret band, Queen Sarah was highly trained and disciplined in the ways of the Ancient Ones. Her face—the forehead now knotted in pain—was clear and beautiful, with a tawny complexion offset by dark ringlets that fell to her shoulders. She opened her wide brown eyes, smiled, and interrupted her meditation to say, "Our Father was with us. It was a great victory."

Taktu untied the top of the queen's cloak and gently moved the soft white muslin undergarment off her shoulder. Zhu Li seemed unperturbed as he took a small packet from inside his belt and unfolded its cloth cover. Carefully, he placed a needle at each of Sarah's eyebrows and turned the thin spikes delicately so as not to inflict pain. A third needle he placed at the queen's chin.

"Tell me when the pain stops," Zhu Li said to Queen Sarah. He allowed these to set a moment, until Sarah told him the pain was gone.

"Good," he replied and went to work bathing the wound and removing the arrowhead with a small blade. All the while he softly chanted, appealing to the Divine Mother he knew from his culture of the Far East. To him, the Heavenly Mother was the manifestation of mercy, compassion, and healing.

Soon the wound was dressed and the queen lay propped on a cushion, sipping hot broth while the others also rested and ate. They would remain in this cavern for at least another day and night. During this time, a scout could make sure that the Huns had indeed departed before the group made its way back up the canyon and into the highlands.

Revived by the easing of pain and the eating of light food, Sarah asked Zhu Li, "What news do you have of our son?"

Zhu Li laughed. "The mighty warrior, little Vima Kadphises? See for yourself!"

The queen's nursemaid, Lariska, stepped forward from the shadows into the ring of campfire light, holding the six-month-old baby in her arms. "Here is your son, my queen."

Sarah's eyes lit up. "Yekte Vima!" she called out, laughing with delight. Sarah cradled her son on her uninjured shoulder. "Did you bring all of our court?" the queen joked, looking at Zhu Li.

"Only the most trusted," he replied, "to help us. And yekte Vima"—little Vima—"wanted to come! How could I refuse? Please, try to sleep."

With her baby at her side and her husband resting next to her, Queen Sarah closed her eyes again.

2

FARAWAY CLASSES

Nazareth, fourteen years after the birth of Jesus

THE NOONDAY SUN SHONE HOTLY ABOVE THE BUSTLING marketplace. From vendors in the dusty square, Mary gathered ingredients for making the flat, round bread her family ate with lentils, spiced vegetables, and other dishes she prepared. Her husband, Joseph, remained at home, working with young Jesus in the carpentry shop that provided a livelihood for the family.

Stopping at a cloth-covered stall, Mary offered a farmer two coins for a portion of grain. The bent old man scooped a hollow gourd into the large, rough-sewn sack of wheat sitting open on the ground. He filled the gourd twice, each time pouring its contents into the cloth pouch hanging from Mary's shoulder. Two little children held onto Mary's robe.

A fine gentleman, obviously of some means, stood at her side and vied for her attention midst the children and the seller.

"Mary, it is time that we plan carefully for the continuation of his education. The Heavenly Father has his time for all things. I will be leaving soon, and he must not miss this opportunity to meet his teacher. Who knows when it will come again?"

"Yes, I know," Mary replied gently to her uncle. "Do you think it is truly the Father's will for him to go away again? Jesus is young. He needs more time with Joseph to learn his trade, and more time to grow into real manhood. I must pray about this. Our Heavenly Father will surely make Jesus' path clear."

Mary wondered if the real reason for her hesitancy was that it was *indeed* his time. Mature and sensitive for her thirty years, she was also a devoted mother. The reality of separating was hard to bear. One of the children with her, a young boy with golden curls, found a stone and threw it, laughing at a mongrel dog skulking around the stalls.

"James!" Mary reprimanded. "It is not right to hurt that poor dog. He has done nothing to you."

The toddler girl at her knee whined, "Mama, I'm hungry."

Mary looked plaintively into the gentleman's face. "Uncle Joseph, perhaps we should talk about this later," she said, sighing and smiling faintly.

"Yes," he responded, relenting for now. "Bring the family to my home tonight for dinner."

"But Jesus will be with us and I don't want him to be troubled."

"It's fine. He will understand."

Mary knew this was true. She nodded and, gathering her pouch, hurried the children home.

THE HOUSE OF JOSEPH OF ARIMATHEA WAS SITUATED on the edge of town. It was always exciting for Jesus and his brother and sister to visit their great-uncle's home because it was full of exotic souvenirs from his travels.

He was a successful merchant who had gone on trips as far as the northern islands across the sea and eastward into India. For most people, these places existed only in the realm of stories. Joseph's house was more than just one of the largest Jewish homes in the area. It was also an elegant show-case of his wares, often visited by the servants of Roman nobility who came to procure handsome furnishings from India or carved marble from Greece. Colorful silk tapestries draped the walls, and rainbows of rich silk fabrics were stacked in neat folds on benches and shelves. Best of all was the thick smell of spices, oils, and precious incense brought back from the markets of foreign lands.

Joseph was generous in giving sizable discounts to the Roman governor, his court in Jerusalem, and to his local representatives in Nazareth. After every journey, Joseph's servants delivered beautiful gifts of gold, jewels, and silks along with an announcement of the arrival of special items that might interest the prefect. These Roman connections were priceless not only for favor in political matters, the least of which was taxes, but also—and most significantly—for the protection of the Roman army. While Joseph had his own servants, he also depended upon the Roman army to afford him safe passage through their lands, both in his own country and around Rome.

Many of Joseph's Jewish friends criticized his familiarity with the Romans, but they could not criticize his devotion to God, nor his donations to the temple in Jerusalem and the synagogues elsewhere. Joseph of Arimathea was known for his piety, fairness, and generosity.

That evening, as the family walked through the labyrinth of twisted byways to reach the great man's house, Jesus reflected on his childhood years under the merchant's care. Joseph and Mary had entrusted this great-uncle with Jesus as a boy, allowing him to escort their child far from home across the sea. The adults agreed that the northern isles would be safer than the vicinities of Egypt or Galilee.

There, on those isles, Jesus had studied with the finest teachers of his time. Even now, the teen could still see himself as a tender seven-year-old, clutching Uncle Joseph's hand while their ship plowed through rough seas. Though determined to study and prepare for his Father's calling, he remembered tears burning his cheeks on the day Joseph of Arimathea returned home, leaving Jesus behind in the foreign land, brave yet bereft of all blood-kin.

In that moment, he could once again smell the porridge cooking in the thatched hut he shared with his elderly tutor. Jesus' stomach churned as he thought of the burly boys who taunted him when he left the sanctity of the hut.

Finally, his body again felt the peace of self-control. The old man had taught him this through long and tedious lessons that were nevertheless enthralling observations of nature, the elements, the plants, animals, and people.

Every morning the tutor and his small, prodigious pupil worshipped the great Father. All day and long into the night they studied the skies, the wind, water, fire, earth, and its inhabitants great and small. Jesus learned to read the faces, emotions, thoughts, and motives of people around him. The boy's mind became sharp and disciplined. Jesus' intuition developed. When Joseph of Arimathea returned for Jesus several years later, he had found a changed boy.

Jesus had returned to Nazareth, continuing his study of Hebrew law, and in a year or two he was astounding the rabbis in the temple in Jerusalem with his knowledge and interpretation of the scriptures.

AT LAST THE SMALL GROUP ARRIVED AT THEIR DESTINATION. Uncle Joseph himself opened wide the heavy wooden double doors with brass ornamentation.

There stood the family before him. Mary held little Miriam in her arms. Her husband stood next to her. He and Joseph of Arimathea were close friends with high regard for each other. Next to Joseph of Nazareth was little James and then Jesus, who stood almost as tall as his father.

"Welcome!" With outstretched arms, Joseph of Arimathea focused his attention on the three children. Jesus was almost fourteen, James was eight, and Miriam was three. "Who will find the hidden treasure?" he teased. Joseph bent over, smiling mischievously at Miriam and James.

A widower, "Uncle Joseph" cherished the three children as his own. He missed them in his long absences, and while careful not to provide them with an overabundance of gifts, this great-uncle took pleasure in delighting the children with special treats and games that he had devised on his trips.

Miriam seriously studied Uncle Joseph's round face and pondered his question about finding the hidden treasure. As Joseph bent over, Miriam took her chubby little hands and placed them on each side of his silvery beard. The three adults and Jesus worked hard to stifle laughs when Miriam looked deeply into her uncle's blue eyes and said slowly with somber inflection, "Uncle Joseph, our good Father *shows* us all things."

Laughing, Joseph placed his hand on the top of her head. "Ah, my wise little Miriam," he said as he crouched next to her, "how can I argue with the truth? All right. I will be just like our good Father when you are seeking his will. I will give you clues to guide you!

"Come close," he said to both James and Miriam. Joseph extended his arms to reach around the two and in a loud whisper announced, *"This* treasure is *alive!* His ancestor played mischief long ago in the Far East and was named Hanuman! You will find him with a mysterious stranger. And"—he winked—"one of his favorite fruits is dates." From the small bag he wore slung across his chest, Joseph took several dates and handed them to the two children. "Now, go find him!"

As the children ran through the familiar house, Uncle Joseph took Mary, Jesus, and Joseph into his main room. Servants came with basins of water for washing. The family members settled onto comfortable cushions around the low table while servants laid flat breads, spicy vegetables, cheese, nuts, and fruits before them. Uncle Joseph spread his hands over the food. "My blessed loved ones, let us pray. Creator of all, bless this food and this company. Guide us in the ways of Abraham to follow thy will. Strengthen the fire in our hearts. Reveal to us thy perfect plan for thy beloved son Jesus."

Jesus fidgeted. *Why the special prayer about me today?* he wondered without asking out loud. He had the uncanny sense that something was about to happen. He stole a quizzical look at Uncle Joseph, then at his parents, and perceived uneasiness in their faces. Were they keeping something from him? Suddenly his appetite faded as he pondered the purpose of this family gathering.

Joseph continued, "So, my nephew, tell me about your studies. Are you still spending a great deal of time in the synagogue?"

"Yes, Uncle," Jesus replied. "The rabbis allow me to come when I want to now, and I try to memorize the Torah and the teachings on the law when I am there." The young man sensed his family would be concerned if he didn't eat. He broke off a piece of bread. His long-fingered hands were at once strong and fine. He nibbled absently as he concentrated on the family members and waited for their conversation to unfold.

Like other men of his Jewish sect in Nazareth, Jesus wore a long white tunic. His face showed only the faintest traces of the beard that would soon frame his pleasant features. Jesus' expressive eyes often flickered with joy and wisdom, and at times a sorrow that neither he nor anyone in his family could explain.

"That is excellent," Joseph exclaimed. "And what do you know of your reputation? Do you know that you are the talk of our people?" he asked, smiling. "And of the Romans?" he added more seriously.

Jesus regarded his great-uncle and without pretense or pride, replied softly, "More people have been gathering when I explain my understanding of the scriptures."

"And have you noticed any Roman guards in the crowds?" Joseph of Arimathea pressed.

Jesus shook his head from side to side. He asked himself why he was feeling more and more restless. It was clear Uncle Joseph had news that would affect him.

Joseph of Arimathea turned to Joseph and Mary. "I tell you, when I came back from my journey, I was accosted by the priests of the temple wanting to learn more about my nephew. The Romans who came to my home were also asking questions. Because he is such a gifted young man, some people are already proclaiming him to be the fulfillment of prophecy and the Messiah they are waiting for. This gives me grave concern for Jesus' safety. My dear ones, in my opinion, there is no time to lose.

"Brother," he addressed Mary's husband, "you were wise to live in Egypt with your family in those early years. Upon your return to Nazareth, and with Jesus studying in the northern isles as a boy, you have all been able to blend in and live peacefully, until now."

"Jesus," Mary said, "perhaps it is time you worked more in your father's business and learned his trade better. You must always have an honest way to support yourself while you do the Almighty's work, even if someday you are meant to be a rabbi. By working more with your father now, there will be less attention paid toward you."

Joseph took the hand of his young wife into his own leathered one. His hair was silvery, yet his body was firm, tan, and strong. Joseph of Nazareth was a master craftsman. He designed intricate furnishings, temple accessories, and inlaid wooden chests with secret compartments, carefully wrought by his staff. His work was much demanded by nobility, even in Egypt. He often meditated alone in his chambers, contemplating prophecy and seeking answers through prayer and study of Hebrew law.

He looked into his wife's face, at her expression of concern. Jesus was her first child, born of prophecy known to the secret Order of Melchizedek, a brotherhood and sisterhood of devout souls steeped in traditions of mysticism and seeking to follow God's will.

Jesus was Mary's only child for several years. The family knew his heritage and his lineage. Because of this, they had gone to great lengths to protect and educate him in the inner ways of the Father. They believed his role was to be a master teacher and prophet. What they didn't know was how God's plan would be revealed.

Jesus' restlessness did not dissipate as the meal progressed. He remembered when he had once been separated from his parents during their pilgrimage to Jerusalem. Then he had thought nothing of the crowded streets or of whether his mother and father would be concerned by his disappearance. He had been overcome by the command of his Heavenly Father to learn more and give more. When at last his parents found him with the rabbis in the temple, Jesus was oblivious to time, and to the need for food and rest. His response was, "I'm doing my Father's work."

Now Jesus' sense of an inner command grew again, and it was caused not only by his great-uncle's interrogation about his more recent activities. Jesus once again felt the burning drive to learn. It was an unquenchable thirst, and although he was powerless to dismiss the feeling, he was hesitant about breaking the news to his family—especially to his incomparable mother.

The young man wrestled with a desire to keep his thoughts to himself, but knew he must speak. He often marveled at his father's diplomacy when dealing with wealthy customers. Joseph could explain his designs and prices with such ease and at just the right moment. The craftsman's opinion was almost always accepted. Jesus, on the other hand, could never withhold a word he felt pressed to say, regardless of the possible effect on the hearer. But he anticipated tonight that his mother might be saddened. He felt the nervous rush of his heartbeat.

"Uncle," Jesus said, breaking the silence, "although I have already studied and learned much, our Father is pressing me to find a still-greater teacher than those who have instructed me already. John and I have talked many late nights about our missions. It is time for me to go and find the one who can instruct and prepare me."

There. It was out. Jesus sucked in a deep breath and felt his heart and stomach calm down.

Mary looked tenderly at her son. She knew from her own experience that the Creator worked in miraculous ways. If her son felt the Father's prompting, she could not deny it. She must encourage Jesus to follow that inner direction. At the same time, Mary was also a wise mother, knowing it was her job as a loving parent to properly instruct and guide her boy. Gently she tested his resolve with her questions.

"Jesus, where will you find your teacher? Do you know who he is? And, our Father is the one who instructs us in all things. Do you need to seek him in faraway places? He is always here with you. There are many rabbis who can continue to teach you.

"And as for your cousin John, his fervor is strong. Only *he* can find God's will for his own path, just as only *you* can listen to the Father for your own inner directions. Others, such as Uncle Joseph, may have ideas about travel to distant and dangerous lands, but only you can discern your Father's calling."

The three men and the woman at the table sat silently, lost in their thoughts.

Finally Joseph of Arimathea spoke.

"My niece, blessed of heaven, you have beheld the face

of an angel, a messenger of the Most High. The Creator as a mother is so strong in your heart that even I feel her defense of her child through you." He turned to Jesus. "Your mother is right. You and John both have holy missions. I believe John will prepare the hearts of men and women for greater understanding, and you, young man, will save them by showing true peace through the inner knowledge of the Almighty in their hearts. How, we do not know. But as your guardians, we all know you must be trained. The Father, with our help, will direct you in your course."

"Yes," said Mary calmly. And, still testing her son's resolve, she added, "This is true. Do not forget there is wisdom right here in Nazareth and beyond in Jerusalem. Already you have been taught a great deal about the ways of devotion and union with the Father."

Joseph of Nazareth nodded silently. He, too, was pained at the thought of Jesus' leaving again. He had a faraway expression on his face, even though he looked only at a tapestry on the opposite wall. He said, "There are more pathways to God in the world than can be found in our little Nazareth or even Jerusalem. The Anointed One is to be a savior and way-shower for the *world*."

Mary rose quietly from her cushion. She sighed. Her heart yearned to assist young Jesus in differentiating between the inner promptings of his Father and the outer influences that could result in wrong choices. Nevertheless, she knew this was his personal test of manhood and discernment. Mary also knew that only in prayer could she find solace and help for her son without being overly protective. He had to follow his own calling.

Still, her obedience to the Creator was intensely painful. Jesus was her beloved son. She had worked hard to train him lovingly in the Father's will, teaching him the laws of her people, kindness, and soul-testing. The inner circle of the secret Order of Melchizedek believed that Jesus was the Messiah and that he had led them lifetimes ago in golden ages upon Earth, long lost to the memories of the people.

The Order believed Jesus had returned to lead all sons and daughters of the Most High. More than that, he would be an example: one man who reminded all people of the Creator's spark burning in their own hearts. He would be the Anointed One—*Christos,* in the Greek language they were familiar with.

Moreover, they believed that Jesus' cousin John was also a prophet walking the earth again, sent to awaken the hearts of the lost sheep who had forgotten their divine heritage. To the Order of Melchizedek, it was not an accident that John came at this time to prepare many for the coming of the Christ.

"I will find the children in the garden so they can have their dinner," Mary said, bowing her head slightly as she left the room.

THE CHILDREN'S DELIGHTED LAUGHTER FLOATED IN FROM the garden as Mary passed along the lattice-covered walkway. The flowering jasmine spread its fragrance in the evening air. Mary stopped in the shadow of a portico that opened into the garden. Hidden in the shadows of the walkway, she sought the attunement of her heart with the Almighty. The palm of her right hand pressed over the gold medallion hanging from her neck. Mary was sensitive to the Signet, a symbol of the light within her. Her hand felt warmth come into it as she pictured the star with its dancing flames. The image danced to life as she imagined the light of the Mother rising from the base of her spine and the light of the Father descending from above to meet in her own heart.

She went deeper into this light and was transported to an altar within. Upon the inner altar of white and rosy light, there burned three living flames, gently pulsating. They intertwined, yet were distinct. One was a brilliant rosy pink, one was a dazzling yellow, and the last was an intense blue. Mary saw herself kneeling in adoration before this living presence of the Divine as she observed a silvery crystal light rising up from the plumes, reminding her of sweet incense on the temple altars.

Transfixed by her vision, Mary silently dropped to her knees, her right hand upon her heart and her left placed over it. "O Father-Mother, my blessed parents and light of all sons and daughters, what is your will for your beloved son? Teach me how to be strong and how to assist him in his mission, *your* mission." As she spoke, Mary felt comforted and reassured of the path ahead.

The plumes of light in her heart intensified. She paused, absorbing the holy silence, and then felt the soft voice of the flame impressing upon her. *Set your sight upon the victory of my son. Keep the vision immaculate, my daughter.*

Mary bowed her head and paused a few more moments to allow this understanding from her Divine Father and Mother to settle within her before the children's laughter in the garden brought her back from her reverie. She rose to her feet, turned the corner, and entered the garden.

"James!" she exclaimed. "What have you there?"

At first, the scene was confusing. In the light of an oil lamp sat James with a small furry creature settled contentedly on the top of his head. It looked like a tiny man. Its long tail hung down over James' shoulder, and its little furry hands pulled apart a date.

The creature quickly savored the bites, its quizzical face looking back and forth between the date and Mary. Miriam sat cross-legged a few feet away, giggling delightedly.

Between the two children stood a small, bald man, scarcely five feet tall. He was naked except for his white loincloth. His dark-brown body looked bony and sinewy, his shoulders slightly stooped. Yet there was a happy disposition about him, and it was clear he enjoyed the delight of the children. The man looked up at Mary and bowed low several times while smiling broadly, revealing missing front teeth. As he bowed, his right hand was tucked in slightly at his waist while his left arm waved in the air at his side. His left hand was gnarled into a claw-like shape with stiff, useless fingers.

"I am Awa," he said. "I come with my little friend, Hanuman." He nodded toward the monkey. "We traveled with Master Joseph from my homeland in the East." He beamed.

"Mama!" James exclaimed. "Look!" The young boy slowly stood from his cross-legged position with Hanuman still balancing on his head. He walked carefully toward his mother. Hanuman, having finished his date, turned a few times on James' head, causing Miriam to laugh all the more. When James was three feet from his mother, Hanuman suddenly leaped to Mary's shoulder.

"Oh!" she gasped, totally surprised yet quickly giving a smile to the friendly creature.

"Hanuman! Come here!" Awa commanded. Immediately the little monkey dropped down, scampered across the garden, jumped up onto Awa's shoulder and peeked shyly from behind Awa's neck. "So sorry," Awa apologized with another round of little bows. Miriam and James' laughter was joined by applause and laughs from behind Mary. She turned to see Jesus, her husband, and her uncle in the portico.

"Good show!" Joseph of Arimathea laughed as he clapped

his hands. Stepping forward to join Mary, he said, "Awa is an excellent translator. Not only can he help me with trade, but he can also help Jesus as we travel through the East. I have already told him much about your son."

Joseph sent the two little ones with the housekeeper to have their dinner and then continued, "Please tell my friends your story, Awa."

Awa scratched his bald head and said, "There is not much to tell, Master. My family in the town of Benares was very poor. We are Sudras, laborers. My father collected refuse, my father's father collected refuse, and I collected refuse. My father collected the refuse in a Brahman household. And so did his father's father. Three times a day he took waste from the master's big house to the faraway field. Some things he could save for our hut.

"One day my little sister, who was two, was caught under the wheels of an oxcart when the ox backed up suddenly. I was only five, but I tried to grab her before the cart came. I was too late. My foot was hurt, but I could still limp to go to my father. My father ran and took my little sister from the ground. Her chest was badly crushed, but he laid her under a tree and cried for help.

"Who was there to help? And why would they help this little one? In my country, people think, 'She is only a girl. Better for the family to lose her than pay a dowry or have another mouth to feed.' Still, we loved her. She was so sweet and beautiful. However, she breathed her last and my father brought her home.

"My mother was away from the hut, gathering scraps of cloth from the tailor to stuff pillows. My father went to find her. Mother came back to call upon the gods for my sister, but my father had to go back to the house of the Brahmans. I was small, but I had to go, too, and help with the slop buckets.

"I liked the house of the Brahman family, but we were not allowed to look into their eyes, walk in their shadows, or look at their food, because that would be unclean. The Brahmans read the sacred words of the Vedas, but we could not read them, or even listen to them, for that would be unclean. I could not help it but to listen a little behind the walls. Sometimes I stopped to listen a lot, though that was dangerous. When you are small, people do not notice you so much.

"It was not a lucky day for my father. He was late because of my little sister's death, and the Brahman's daughter had become sick. The slop jar was full and smelly. The Brahman and his wife were very angry and upset. I think the daughter was very, very sick." He nodded his head back and forth on his neck and clucked as if coming to a new revelation.

"'Why have you not come?' they shouted at my father. 'You are lazy and stupid and you are causing our daughter's death. Take this slop jar!' they shouted at me. 'We will deal with this stupid insect for his crimes.' I was very afraid. I didn't know what I should do."

Though the story was fifty years in the past, Awa's face winced in pain. He would have wrung his hands, but instead he grasped the stiff, claw-like fingers of his left hand.

"My father nodded to me, so I carefully picked up the jar. It was very heavy and I was shaking and still limping, but I did not spill a drop. I went outside and as I was leaving the courtyard, I heard the shouts of the Brahman, 'Take this beast out behind the wall. I will be there myself.' I could not turn around for I might accidentally look at the Brahman or his men and make it worse for my father. When I got behind the courtyard wall and was on my way to the field, I heard the lash and my father's screams.

"I did my best to empty the pot and scrub it clean in a little stream, thinking the better I did, the better it would go for my father. I ran back and went the way of the servants in order to replace the slop jar. I called to a household servant, 'Master, master! It is very, very clean!' He looked at me, nodded, and told me to go home now, that I was too little and his master and mistress did not want to see me in the house again.

"I went home and told my mother what had happened. That night we found my father's body behind the courtyard wall."

Awa paused and took a breath. "And so," he said, "it was very hard for my mother and me. She gathered rags and begged. I also begged and looked for work gathering refuse in the marketplace. The other refuse workers threatened me and said they already had this place for their own work. My mother became very thin. Her teeth and hair fell out, and finally she died when I was six. Some time later, a merchant said to me that his refuse worker had died so I could work for him, but that I was too little to be paid, so he would give me bread if I worked hard.

"That was a good job," Awa said, smiling his toothless grin. "I could see and learn so many things in the marketplace, even while I was gathering refuse. I slept on the ground outside the merchant's stall and all the time I worked, I listened. Over the years, I learned to speak the tongues of the traders who came to visit my master. They were different, and didn't know our ways.

"But at last my master died and I was again without work. One of my friends in the marketplace was a beggar nearing the end of his life. He had this monkey, Hanuman, who was like his child. The monkey helped him beg." Awa snapped his fingers. Furry little Hanuman jumped down from Awa's shoulder, ran behind him and grabbed a wooden bowl, then ran to Mary, Joseph, and the others, holding up the bowl. Joseph of Nazareth laughed and dropped a small copper coin into it. Hanuman automatically and jerkingly bowed low and scampered back to Awa while the others laughed.

"You see," said Awa, "he is a very good worker! That's because—" here the story-teller paused and lowered his voice to a whisper feigning secrecy—"he is *more* than a monkey."

Awa raised his voice for emphasis. "He is a nature spirit!" he proudly announced, and then added thoughtfully, "or maybe even a god in this furry form."

The old man surveyed his audience, sensing disbelief. "It's true, I tell you. Hanuman knows when there is danger long before I do. He warns me one way or another. His antics make people laugh. He lifts their hearts. No, this little monkey is not just a pet." Awa's emotions drove him on as he turned to the creature of his attention. "He is a hero, a warrior, a comic, a merchant! And he is my only son," he concluded wistfully. "Hanuman even introduced me to Master Joseph by running to him in the marketplace. Who would do that but a nature spirit? That was a great day for me because Master Joseph asked me to work for him and told me much about Master Jesus, whom I call 'Master Issa' in my language." With this comment, he bowed respectfully toward them all three times.

Mary, sitting on a low garden wall, asked, "What do you know about my son?"

With reverence, Awa replied, "I know that he has come from Heaven and from ancient times to teach us and save us from our karma of dark days."

Mary pondered the meaning of Awa's strange words.

"Master Joseph told me," he continued, "that Jesus must go to my land to find his teacher, prepare for his work, and speak to my people. I would serve him and Master Joseph with my life."

Jesus observed Awa thoughtfully before asking, "And your hand? What happened to your left hand?"

"Oh this...." Awa looked down and continued. "One day when I was about thirty, I was discovered in the bushes outside the temple, listening to the Vedas, the sacred scriptures. In my bad luck, a Brahman came out to relieve himself and saw me. He was outraged, called the temple guards, and accused me of looking upon him in his privacy.

"They grabbed me and debated whether to kill me on the spot. The gods had mercy and one of those officials recognized me and said, 'He is the refuse collector for a wealthy merchant who should keep a better watch over him. We will take his left hand and send him back. Let that be a lesson.' So they immediately bound me and heated pine resin to boiling. With a big sword one of them struck at my hand with one blow, but it didn't sever completely. 'Never mind,' another said, 'it is a good enough cut to make it useless. Waste no more time on him but stop the bleeding and send him back to his master to keep him out of trouble.'

"When they plunged my almost-severed hand into the boiling resin, I passed out and knew nothing until I woke up behind my master's stall with my hand and wrist bound in rags. When he saw I was awake, my master slapped my face and told me I had brought much shame upon his house and never to go near the temple again. He said I was lucky he did not throw me into the street like refuse."

All were quiet.

JESUS' THOUGHTS SWIRLED AND HE TOOK A DEEP BREATH. Awa's story had moved him profoundly. He felt impelled to be about his Father's work.

The weight of his choice rested heavily upon him. Questions bounded into his mind. Should he travel with Uncle Joseph and leave behind his family? Would his mother grieve over his long absence? Would his journey to a distant land be futile, or would he find someone who could lead him even closer to his Father? Through all the painful questions, a persistent inner pull made him feel the only answer was to go forward.

Mary knew the difficult choice before her son. "Dear Lord," she prayed silently, "truly you have set your flame into the hearts of many who by outer appearances are well disguised. Have you sent this one and his little friend to lead my son to find his teacher?"

When Jesus turned to her, Mary was not surprised, having become accustomed to her son's answering her unspoken prayers.

"You are wise, Mother," he said. "Indeed, the Creator places his flame within his children everywhere they are scattered, no matter what skins they wear. And then he calls them to their divine purposes."

"Yes, my son," Mary replied as she brought back the vision that the soft voice had asked her to hold immaculate. "We honor all those who will help you in your quest.

"Come," she said to Awa, "let us rejoin the children and all finish our dinner together."

Suddenly there was a great pounding at the heavy front doors on the other side of the portico.

"The Messiah is in here!" they heard a woman scream. "I saw him go in!"

"Joseph of Arimathea!" male voices called, accompanied by more pounding. "Let us in! Introduce us to the one who has come to save us from the Romans and the Emperor!"

"Zealots," Joseph of Arimathea whispered. "And noisy ones. What are they thinking? They believe the Messiah comes to save us from worldly politics!" He shook his head. "Well, do they want all the guards of Rome to come down upon Jesus and all of us? There is no time to lose. Jesus, Awa, and I must leave the city with my trading caravan tomorrow before sunrise. Pray that no guards have heard their cries tonight. Awa, do what you can to divert these people. Mary, gather the children now. You must all go out the back way. I will send my servant to accompany you home and come back for Jesus in the middle of the night."

As they hurried away, Awa dropped his monkey down

over the wall into the midst of the small crowd.

"What is it?" a voice cried in alarm. The group broke into a small circle around the chattering monkey. Awa opened the front double doors. The people were even more surprised to see this strange little brown-skinned man—with a crumpled hand, a toothless smile, wearing only a loincloth—greet them in the doorway to the house of Joseph of Arimathea.

"I am Awa," he said in Aramaic, which the Jews spoke. He smiled and bowed. "I am the one you seek. Hanuman and I will save you from your troubles." Awa snapped his fingers three times and Hanuman scampered up onto his shoulder.

Joseph of Arimathea appeared tall behind Awa. "This is my guest from the East," he said. "I hope you don't think he is going to save you from Rome. But you are welcome to come in, my friends, and he will certainly entertain you for the evening and make you forget about Rome for a while!"

The small group stood dumbfounded as Joseph stepped aside to make way for them to enter. Finally, blinking, one of the men said, "There must have been some mistake. Excuse us for bothering you, Master Joseph." Turning to the others, he said, "Let's go," and they emptied into the quiet night muttering to one another about how Joseph of Arimathea seemed to become stranger with every passing day.

In the dark back alleys of Nazareth, the family of five and Joseph of Arimathea's servant noiselessly passed through the town. Mary's heart pounded. Jesus would leave before the sun came up. This mother did not know when or where she would ever see her son again. All but the little ones felt the poignancy of the impending separation, though they did not speak of it.

Mary once again mentally repeated the words that had entered her heart earlier in the evening. "Set your sight upon the victory of my son. Keep the vision immaculate, my daughter." She checked her strong emotions before they could well up inside of her.

It would be seventeen years before Mary would once again embrace Jesus. Joseph of Nazareth would never see him again.

3

SEEDS OF WHEAT

Near Kapisa, Afghanistan, the same year

> *Ah Shamballa, far away,*
> *Your sheep are scattered.*
> *Where are they now, O Ancient Ones?*
> *Our true leader, Ancient of Days,*
> *Come, lead us to Shamballa again.*
>
> *Ah Shamballa, far away,*
> *We long to see your hidden treasures.*
> *Where is the Sacred Flame kept now?*
> *Show us once more your secret cave.*
>
> *Ah Shamballa, ever close,*
> *All I do is close my eyes*
> *To find my Father and my Mother*
> *In my own true secret cavern.*
> *Lead me to Shamballa again.*

ISSA

VIMA KADPHISES WAS TEN TODAY. THE STORY OF HIS INFANCY had been recounted to him often. He had been brought to his mother in a hidden cave after the Kushans had retrieved their horses from a Hun encampment. Vima's family thought it was an appropriate beginning to a life that promised to be one of adventure.

The young prince learned to sing his people's traditional folk songs about Shamballa in the strong and free style of the Kushan horsemen. He sang them as the small royal caravan made its way back north, traveling along the Indus River and then west through the mountains.

"Maybe they will stop calling me 'yekte'—little—Vima today," Vima thought as he looked ahead to see his father, King Vima Taktu, on a magnificent black steed. The boy's curly golden-brown hair crowned a young face, wide and with round red cheeks. He had his father's blue eyes.

"Now I am old enough to demonstrate my weapons," he reasoned. Shouting, "Ooohpaah!" he turned his brown mare and galloped to the back of the caravan in search of his young friend, Sanum. Vima twirled his sword high above his head, imitating what he had learned in his lessons. His legs barely reached the middle of his mare's belly. Still, he rode well, gripping with his knees and balancing his weight in the fine leather saddle. He was dressed in soft, tan woolen trousers and a brown tunic with a royal blue sash that billowed behind him as his horse raised clouds of dust on the road.

The caravan was almost home after a long journey to bring back seeds of wheat for their people. Taktu had personally led the caravan from their city of Kapisa, high in a mountain valley where they had settled after the Huns pushed them out of northwest Asia long ago. The essential seeds would create a stable farming life and assure the food supply of his people.

In India the royal party had met with princes to trade horses: strong, beautiful animals that were the pride of royalty and priceless in war. These mighty stallions and sturdy mares were much larger than the horses of the subcontinent. Some of the mares served as smaller packhorses, carrying loads on the return portion of their trip.

Although the great stories of Taktu's homeland took place long before his birth, he believed in them deeply. And like all his people, the ruler carried on the tradition of the songs of the Ancient Ones, whom the Kushan believed once lived in the heavenlike place named Shamballa, now lost. The beautiful, fabled city was made of white marble, shining in the midst of a shallow blue sea and connected to the shore by graceful stone bridges. The inhabitants were masters of many arts, devoted to Appakke Nakte, and dedicated to the noble virtues of peace and enlightenment.

But that was so many generations ago. Now, no one knew what had become of the city, the sea, or the inhabitants. All that remained was a few individuals—known to each other as members of the secret Order of Melchizedek—who mastered some of the ancient ways of astronomy, invocation, commanding the elements, and healing. Taktu and his wife were two of these.

And Taktu worried about Vima Kadphises, his only son, who took even less interest than his own generation in meditating upon the inner flame, the source of a wise leader's power. That was the very reason Taktu took the risk of bringing him on this long journey. His son would meet the princes of India, visit the foreign temples, and find holiness with the wise ones there.

And how else would his son learn trade, diplomacy, and the cultures of so many foreign paths? Taktu had only persuaded Queen Sarah to let Vima come along by convincing her of the wisdom of his plan and promising to be home by the boy's birthday.

Now as Taktu heard the war cry and looked over his shoulder to see his son galloping to the end of the caravan, wildly twirling a sword over his head in abandon of all discipline, he sighed and wondered about the future of his land and its people.

"Sanum! Sanum!" Vima called as he reined in near his friend and a swirl of dust floated around him. "I challenge you!"

"You challenge a *girl*?" Sanum laughed and pushed back the soft brown mantle over her head. Sanum was twelve.

Her father, Wenta, was Taktu's chief counselor. When she had learned that her friend, Vima, was going on the caravan, she pleaded with her father to let her come along. Children were never allowed on trading caravans, so why should Vima get to go and not her?

There had been much deliberation in the royal court. All recognized that Vima and Sanum got along famously. They both studied under tutors of astronomy, war skills, language, music, arts, and animal husbandry. In fact, Sanum was usually much better than Vima in their classes, perhaps because of her age, or perhaps because of her intuition. She often helped Vima with his lessons, even the lessons of war skills. Sanum recognized that the sword challenge came because Vima was ten today. It was the prince's right to try his weapons.

Sanum broke from the line of horses and wrapped her fingers around her sword's hilt, pulling it from its saddle scabbard. "Ooohpaah!" she whooped in response to the prince, raising her sword high. Small white teeth glistened behind her rosy lips. Sanum's tan complexion vexed her mother, who thought women of high rank should stay out of the sun. Straight brown hair flowed to the girl's shoulders.

Vima and Sanum drew their horses side by side for a parry, as they had often done in practice. Sanum automatically brought the focus of her attention into her heart, as she had been taught by her master. Vima, full of excitement, had forgotten his lessons of intuition and self-control. Sanum anticipated his wild cry and the drop of his arm above her. She easily deflected his attempted blow, guiding his arm back behind him with her sword.

Vima became angry. It was not possible to lose on his birthday. Sanum intuited his thoughts and for a split second considered letting him win the next parry.

The horses pranced in a circle around each other. Vima drove at Sanum. In one movement, she and her horse swept to the side, and yekte Vima was forced to rein in abruptly before running into the slow-moving caravan.

By now the weary travelers at the rear of the caravan had stopped for the entertainment; they laughed and cheered. Ignoring the activities behind him, Taktu rode on with his emissaries. Unexpectedly an inner prompting burst through his thoughts about his son. The message was: "Look back!"

Swiveling around in his saddle, Taktu saw the children's skirmish just as his son was about to collide with the caravan. Horses whinnied and reared. Taktu's attention easily could have rested on this boisterous scene, which was disrupting the progress of the caravan. But there was a cloud of billowing brown dust on the left side of the caravan, and a flash of metal. The spear points, with their small fluttering red banners, dredged up an indelible memory. This was a Hun raiding party.

The Huns hated the Kushans and envied their leader for his wealth of strong, large horses that could be used in war.

They feared his potential conquest of greater lands, and despised his determination to never submit.

At first startled by the sight of the enemy, Taktu felt his heart pound. He instinctively took a deep, calming breath, bringing his mind into focus and centering his thoughts on the flame within. "Appakke Nakte, help us!" he petitioned quietly. Swinging his horse around, Taktu signaled to his traveling party, crying out those sacred words as an invocation and alarm.

The emergency call drew instantaneous reaction. The caravan stopped. A split second of eerie silence followed as guards and merchants alike grasped the emergency. Vima and Sanum froze, and a shiver of fear shot through their bodies. Sanum quickly placed her thoughts on Appakke Nakte. Her horse stepped near to Vima's mare. "Your heart," she whispered. Staring ahead, Vima unconsciously grabbed the gold medallion hanging from his neck. His thumb passed over the Signet and he felt peace as his mind became one with the center of his being.

The moment of silence was broken by the haunting war cries of the Huns, who saw they were no longer a surprise. The raiding party of 150 men on horseback outnumbered the caravan of merchants and guards by three to one. The Huns split and galloped to each end of the line.

Caravan guards immediately circled around the line and formed their human shield. The Kushans traveled with these warriors, who were prepared for bandits and skirmish attacks, but the size of this marauding party was surprising and overwhelming. Never before had Huns ventured this far south in pursuit of the Kushan leader.

Hun arrows flew. Taktu raised his arm, and the Kushans drew their bows. The volley flew over the grass. The Kushans were well aware that the Huns wore armor. A Kushan guard, with calm precision, shot his arrow through the throat of an advancing Hun warrior.

The first victory of their enemy enraged the Huns. They intensified their piercing cries and pressed harder, close enough now to thrust their spears. Kushan swords flashed.

Taktu shouted to the captain of the caravan, "The prince!" Some of his men circled back to look for Vima and Sanum.

Vima could not be found. Moments before, he had surveyed the scene in a flash. He saw all the players positioned strategically. By instinct he focused his gaze upon an imposing figure seated on a large roan stallion. It was the leader, dressed in the fine armor and helmet of a Hun general. This was one of the ruthless fighters who populated his father's stories and many of his war-skill teacher's lessons.

The leader observed the engagement. Vima could see the general sneer as he rubbed the tip of his spear with a red cloth. Hun poison—Vima recognized it immediately from his lessons.

The general finished his work and calmly pulled at his long, thin moustache. "You barbarians are putrid," he hissed. "I've waited ten years, but now you will pay, king of the stable boys, for humiliating me with your night visit. I will finish you. And with you go your people." The leader clearly felt smug satisfaction at the near-fulfillment of his conquest.

Vima saw his father at the head of the partially circled caravan, fighting two men. He saw the menacing general slowly circle to the outside of the skirmish, moving toward his father, clearly waiting for his prey to tire. Vima's thoughts locked onto the dark aura of this adversary, and he ducked his head low against the mane of his horse as the general looked up in his direction.

The flash of the boy's observation was over. Without hesitation, he broke from the circle and galloped away from the caravan, keeping low to his mare. He clucked to her encouragingly, as his mother had taught him when he was still a toddler. The bay's ears perked up and her nostrils flared, as she understood some secret inner communion with her young rider.

They swept around far to the rear of the raiding party, unnoticed by all engaged in combat, and stopped a hundred yards behind the Hun general. The horse and prince were motionless.

"Appakke Nakte, I am your son," he whispered and felt the words fill him with courage. His right hand tightly gripped his sword and the other relaxed on the reins of the bay. Vima clucked gently and his horse moved forward, slowly at first and then faster and faster until only a horse length from the general.

Loudly, Vima intoned the special words his father had taught him to strengthen his connection with God: "I AM THAT I AM!" Many times, even in his brief ten years, he had authoritatively decreed this name in practice, calling upon the presence of Appakke Nakte, but never in the reality of combat. Even in the heat of this moment, he couldn't help but be surprised at the intense and shattering strength of the sound.

The general's arm was drawn back to thrust the poisoned spear at Taktu. Vima's cry threw him off as he jerked to see what threat was closing in on his left. Though the general's face remained cauterized in its fierce expression, his eyes widened at the sight of this small, laughable adversary with the royal blue sash.

This hesitation sufficed. With his attention riveted on the general, Vima drove forward and plunged his sword into the open spot of armor below the general's armpit.

The general made no sound. He fixed a deathly and hateful stare directly upon the boy and, gathering all his strength, hurled the poisoned spear at Vima.

The mare's nostrils flared and her attentive ears perked forward as she wheeled to the side and back in response to

Vima's retrieving the bloody sword. Though the general's spear had missed Vima's heart, it had ripped through the side of his tunic, scraping the boy's flesh, and the force of it knocked Vima from his horse. The bay mare called out to her master plaintively and became engulfed in the confusion of nearby fighting men.

The general drew a long, thick sword from its scabbard and prepared to finish this puny heir of the royal Kushan family. He raised his sword to throw it daggerlike.

"Vima! Here! Come!" Sanum, on her horse, had circled behind Vima. The powerfully hurled sword hit the ground with full force as Vima scrambled to the side and reached for Sanum's outstretched arm. Putting his foot in her stirrup, the young prince swung onto the back of her steed and the pair raced toward safety.

Incredulous Hun fighters were torn between chasing the two children and chasing their prime target, the Kushan king. Vima's father and the general decided for them, as Taktu thrust again into the unsettled men. The general shouted his last fierce command to seize the king and, with a penetrating look of hatred, fell from his horse.

Sanum and Vima raced back around the heaviest combat to retreat behind Taktu. Hun men broke away and chased after them. One, then two arrows flew audibly by Vima's head. "Ten-year birthday celebration for a prince!" Vima shouted in Sanum's ear. She smiled silently, proud of the prince's determination to save his father, but swept up in their wildly driven attempt to save their own lives. Her fingers whitened around the reins as she nodded, bent down and drove her horse faster.

As Vima and Sanum drew close behind Taktu, they saw another billowing brown dust cloud arise from the left. "My God, more Huns!" Vima thought, stunned.

The rolling cloud drifted upward, and Sanum and Vima could see underneath the dust what looked like the delicate legs of a hundred horses. Quickly the upper layers of the dust cloud settled, and the leader appeared in splendor, wearing a brilliant white tunic and a violet turban. The other men in the company wore headdresses of white or patterned cloth fixed by a dark band around their foreheads.

The small army galloped straight into the battle. Taktu and his captain, seeing the colors and apparel, realized that these were Persian allies.

Immediately the violet-turbaned leader and two of his men were at Taktu's side, while others moved around Sanum and Vima or rode into the ongoing fight. Two of the Huns attacking Taktu were struck down and lay groaning on the field.

Taktu recognized the man at his side as his boyhood friend, Caspar, now a Persian ruler. His comrade's brilliant teeth flashed from his dark, bearded face as his lips parted in the strain of combat. Caspar rode a small, alert Arabian horse with flared nostrils and an arched tail.

Caspar was Taktu's cohort when they were Vima's age. Taktu's father, Kajula Kadphises, left his son in Persia with this young royal member of the Order of Melchizedek to study astronomy and the many skills that teachers now tried to impart to Taktu's son. As youth, Taktu and Caspar roamed the hills on their horses and wandered the palace in endless pursuit of adventure and misadventure—scattering herds of goats, sneaking into the royal Persian banquets to watch the entertainment, annoying the Zoroastrian priests with their constant boyish antics, setting false alerts for the guards and fighting them in mock battle.

The Kushans and Persians continued their pursuit of the Huns, who were now falling back in the face of fresh defenses. Bodies lay around the caravan and a remnant of the Hun men turned to retreat, speeding off across the valley. The Persians started in pursuit. "Let them go," Caspar called to his men. "They are done."

Quiet returned to the valley, where tufts of yellow-green grass grew on each side of the dirt trail. This portion of the trade route crossed a treeless expanse. Jagged, snow-encrusted mountains rose on both sides of the valley. A river flowed alongside the southern mountains. The Huns had approached from a pass in the closest range to the north. No doubt they were retreating to a temporary encampment there. They must be driven back. Next year, this valley would wave with wheat to make Bactria the Kushans' central home, a place from which the people could push far beyond and become a dominant civilization.

The two kings took in the losses as they leaned back in their saddles. Caspar returned his sword to its scabbard. "It's a good thing I learned to read astronomy and your mind, you goat, or I might not have made it here," he said.

"I am pleased you accepted my invitation to Vima's royal birthday celebration," Taktu said with a wry smile, knowing his old friend understood his true gratitude without needing further words. They urged their horses along the line of the caravan.

Hun bodies lay in the grass. Several Kushan warriors were also dead. Forlorn riderless horses from both sides stood by, whinnying.

The bay mare picked her way closer to the caravan. Vima slid off Sanum's horse. The impact caused him to feel his wound, and though only a graze, he realized that the poison could be fatal. He felt nauseated and his side throbbed. He was light-headed.

He mounted his own mare and she nibbled at a tuft of grass. A warm breeze ruffled her mane.

A strong hand grabbed Vima's shoulder. Vima turned to see his father. Taktu's red beard and cropped hair, with just the slightest interweavings of gray, glistened in the sun. Vima's injury had not yet registered on him.

"My son, meet my old friend, Caspar, royal ruler from Persia. Both of you saved my life today. Caspar, my son is no longer 'little' Vima. He is Vima Kadphises, and one day he will follow me and be King Kadphises."

Vima grew more dizzy and swayed in his saddle. Taktu steadied his son and the emperor's expression of exhausted victory changed to one of grave concern.

4

HOME FIRES

Near Kapisa on the battlefield, the same day

DESPITE HIS GRAVE CONCERN ABOUT HIS SON'S CONDITION, Taktu had to lead. "Gather our wounded men and all the horses," he commanded. The skirmish was over, but weapons and prisoners remained to be dealt with.

"Help me with Vima," Taktu ordered as he motioned a young man to ride closer. "The prince may be seriously injured. A graze, but the Huns use poison and the spearhead was intended for me." The young man, Zhu Ying, hurried to Vima's side.

Zhu was the eighteen-year-old son of Zhu Li, who had welcomed the royal Kushan party in the hidden cave after their raid on the Hun encampment years before. Tall and lithe, the young man shunned his family's traditional Chinese attire and adopted the Kushan dress of woolen trousers and tunic. His dark hair hung straight to the middle of his back, and he tied a yellow band around his forehead, drawing a horizontal dimension to his long, thin face.

Like his father, Zhu was an able fighter and a linguist, speaking Chinese, Tokharian, and Aramaic. Also like his father, Zhu was highly regarded for his healing skills.

More than six months ago when the caravan left for India, the elder Zhu had stayed at home to tend to Queen Sarah, who announced that she was with child—the second for Taktu and Sarah.

Young Zhu sat on his horse facing Vima, who remained on his mare. As Zhu tore the side of the prince's tunic to view the wound, a rush of memory came to his young patient. Vima was back in the older man's apothecary at age four with twelve-year-old Zhu watching over him. A small, cloth-covered window high in the clay wall allowed only a small amount of light into the room. Wooden drawers were stacked from floor to ceiling, the face of each drawer perfectly square and approximately one-hand tall and wide with a metal handle in the middle. Above each handle, simple characters labeled the drawer's contents.

Free spaces of wall had drawings of the human body with lines to show the flow of chi and dots at strategic points. Other drawings were elaborate diagrams of trees and herbs, annotated with their uses.

A low table, completely packed with thick crocks painted with Chinese characters, squatted in the center of the room. Vima's chubby hand reached to take the lid from a blue-glazed pot.

"Curious cat?" Zhu smiled and laughed. With the lid ajar, a pungent smell wafted into the room. Vima looked inside.

"Eew! What are those?" His nose crinkled as he looked at the pickled creatures.

"Sea urchins," Zhu answered. "These have been brought very far. They're good for strong sicknesses."

Vima opened another lid, discovering pickled snakes, and another, finding dried mushrooms.

Finally, the elder Zhu, holding a bowl and pestle, came out from his living quarters behind the apothecary. Carefully he shook powder from the bowl and wrapped it in a small square of green silk. "Here," he said to his son, "take this to Queen Sarah and tell her to mix it with a few drops of water and put it on the king's wound."

Vima would never forget the magical room and the mysterious cures that came from it.

THE SKIN AROUND VIMA'S WOUND WAS RED FROM THE TAINT of poison. Zhu rubbed some powdery paste thickly over it.

"You may feel sick. When we arrive home, I'll apply a new poultice. I think you were protected by your god. The salve will draw out some of the poison." The wound was painful, but Zhu's paste had a soothing effect.

After Vima received Zhu's care, he and Sanum rode with others from the caravan to bring together the animals.

Other members of the caravan stripped the dead adversaries of their armor and any weapons or valuables. The injured Kushans were hoisted onto pack mares, and the group advanced forward again. Zhu rode up and down the crowd, checking on his patients. Caspar rode beside Taktu, with Vima and Sanum behind.

"I came for your son's birthday," Caspar said, "but there is another birthday you should know about. It is one of the main reasons for our meeting tonight with the other members of the Order. You remember the portents of fourteen years ago?"

Taktu nodded. Almost fourteen years ago, all the members of the Order had received notice, by special couriers, of the impending sign in the heavens and its meaning.

One night a courier had arrived at Taktu's small palace, which the caravan was now approaching. The dark-skinned stranger was dressed in the rags of a nomad and was old, with gray hair and missing teeth. A crooked ankle forced him to lean heavily on his staff.

When this foreigner and his bleating charges were noticed at the edge of Kapisa, the shepherds were curious and a crowd gathered. Guards saw the commotion and the unusual man in the middle of it. Many times Taktu had warned his men to be vigilant of possible spies. As a precaution, the king's warriors brought the shepherd to the royal court.

The simple, cavernous meeting room held a raised

platform, two-hands high, in the center of the far wall. Low wooden tables, with cushions for seating, awaited councils and hearings. Oil lamps burned on the tables and threw elongated shadows on the whitened clay walls.

Soldiers surrounded the nomad in the center of the room. Questioning him was difficult, since the man responded neither to Aramaic nor Tokharian.

Taktu, wearing his wool cloak in the cool night, entered the circle of men. While the guards carried on a lively discussion about the visitor, Taktu heard a projected whisper come from the shepherd: "Appakke Nakte."

Without showing surprise, Taktu turned. Was this foreigner simply a wanderer? Why would he have traveled so far from home? Or, was this a messenger of the Order of Melchizedek? Taktu tried to be aware of his inner direction. What was the right step here?

He quietly moved directly in front of the shepherd, stopping no more than a foot away. "Stand back," he told his men.

Taktu peered sternly into the shepherd's face and raised his voice.

"You are a fool. You have come uninvited into our territory. What makes you think you can enter Kushan land?" As he ranted, Taktu walked around the disheveled figure, who looked intimidated and quietly watched the king's mouth.

"For your indiscretion, you must either explain yourself

or leave us five sheep. Where is your family? What are you doing here?"

The exhausted old man swayed, lost his balance, and lunged into the king. As the guards pushed forward to separate them, Taktu felt a scroll of leather slip into his hand.

Without dropping his stern expression, Taktu drew his hand back into his cloak and slid the message into his sash. His left arm pushed against his strange guest.

"Take him to the fields," the king commanded. "Separate five sheep out for our people and send him on his way. Take care to do him no harm," he added. "This man is a simple wanderer."

The stranger bowed low with the palms of his hands pressed together before him and, smiling faintly, said, *"Om Tat Sat Om."* From his travels to India, Taktu recognized the Sanskrit expression for "I AM THAT I AM."

Taktu returned to his chambers where he and Sarah examined the blue seal on the scroll. The Signet was pressed into the wax. He broke the seal and unrolled the leather.

In Aramaic it read, "IN THE WEST, THE GOLDEN SUN SHINES BRIGHTLY."

The pair realized that prophecy was unfolding. From the message, they knew that the long-hoped-for avatar had been born in the land far to the west.

CASPAR BROKE INTO THE KING'S THOUGHTS. "I WENT TO see the avatar, you know, with Melchior and Balthazar. I cannot describe what we felt when we came into the presence of this child and his parents. I thought we were lifted into another world. We sent word throughout our lands that this family was to be protected.

"We were naive. Herod leapt into action. Even today the authorities will stop at nothing to eradicate any possibility of a new leader rising among the people in the Roman empire.

"After we left the child, Herod sent his soldiers throughout the land to kill every male infant." Caspar sighed heavily.

"It was Herod who told us to go to Bethlehem and report back what we learned so that he could worship.

"We followed the sign in the sky and our inner direction, found the child, and offered him our gifts. Before it was time for us to return, God warned us in a dream not to go back to Herod. We returned to our homes by another route, and Herod's carnage began. The holy family, however, escaped to another land. And now I come to you fourteen years later."

Caspar looked up. "My friend," he said, "do you ever wonder how a child becomes an avatar who will teach the world?"

"By the power of Appakke Nakte," Taktu replied.

"Yes, of course. Nevertheless, an avatar also comes with a body like you and me. He must start from the very beginning, learning to eat, walk, and talk and being trained again in the laws of Melchizedek. He may have innate wisdom and compassion, but without training the seed of greater things may remain dormant. The boy I saw as a baby in Bethlehem will need his training, Taktu. But we will talk about that more tonight."

THE TOWN OF KAPISA CAME INTO SIGHT. IN THE FRONT quadrant, behind the protective wall, thick black smoke rose against the blue sky.

A small group of riders galloped toward the caravan, never breaking stride until the lead man pulled to a halt before them, dropped from his horse, and on one knee bowed before the king.

"Peace," said Taktu gravely. This was not the greeting he had expected for the birthday celebration of his son and the return of the caravan. The smoke in the town loomed ominously in the sky. "Speak. What is your message?"

The breathless rider said, "Master, there has been a battle in our town. A deadly party struck us this morning. We have driven them out and captured or killed most of the attackers, but there have been losses. Their goal was to assassinate our queen. We believe they knew that you were not there."

Taktu felt the heaviness of more news, yet unspoken, hanging in the air. He didn't want to ask his real question.

"Who were they?"

"Huns, Master."

"The attack...?"

The man stared at his feet.

"The attack...?" Taktu asked again, louder, as he watched the black smoke.

"It was successful for them, Master."

No! Unspeakable anguish ripped through Taktu's mind. There was no need for further questions. He drove on and the others followed in fast pursuit.

As they approached the gates to Kapisa, they saw people running and shouting to one another, and knew that all had been chaotic a short while before. A ring of soldiers guarded three men lying face down in the dust of the open square, their hands bound tightly behind their backs and their feet spread out and bound to a wooden bar. "These are the living ones," the messenger explained. "We waited for your return to deal with them."

Taktu turned from the square to the burning granary. Men and women had been drawing buckets of well water and passing them hand-to-hand down a line to the blaze. Now they all stood by and watched the flames lick the last of the building.

"This was the diversion," the messenger went on. "When the fire started in the granary, everyone ran to put it out. They didn't hear or see what was happening at the royal house in bold daylight. The attack was well planned."

Taktu rode to the royal compound. Three Kushan guards lay dead at the open gate in the front wall. Worse still was the wall.

On the top of it was the head of Zhu Li. Taktu dismounted and took a step forward to remove the head and restore the honor of his loyal friend.

He felt a hand on his arm. Young Zhu Ying was at his side.

"He is my father," Zhu said in a tone of controlled emotion.

Taktu nodded.

Zhu gritted his teeth. It was the only way he knew to keep from screaming. His eyes burned and his hands shook as he removed his tunic, silently went to the wall, and wrapped his father's head in the garment. He carefully covered the face and cradled his burden like one holds an infant.

The elder Zhu Li had taught his son many things, but above all he had taught him to hide his true emotions, no matter how painful. "In this way," the older man advised, "you will always have the advantage. Enemies will never know your next move, and friends will consider you extremely reliable.

"Especially fight rage. It will consume a person. And, you must never lose face."

"I don't care," Zhu now inwardly shouted back to the phantom in his mind. "You are my father and you are gone."

Nevertheless, he bore the shock and pain without showing his grief. "I will make you proud, Father, at your death.

I will make you proud," he told himself stoically. Zhu thought he could feel a return current of approval. From where? "Let me see you!" his heart cried.

Taktu watched Zhu walk away, knowing that the heaviness he felt in his own heart was the beginning of the grief to come. Quietly he entered the gate and strode through the courtyard.

Two guards, their throats slit, lay in the courtyard. Taktu thought they must have been taken by surprise. They were of the royal family's guards, masters of their weapons.

He saw the body of Zhu Li in a corner of the courtyard. He thought of his companion in the Order of Melchizedek fighting until death was unavoidable and then allowing peace to settle in his heart.

He heard wails coming from the house and followed the sounds into the royal bedchamber.

Sarah was lifeless on the bed, where she had been placed by her two attendants, who now knelt crying at her side.

Her face was still beautiful, with a slight furrow in her brow and an out-of-place look of peace created by her slightly upturned lips. A fine white cloth covered the queen's body to her shoulders. Her delicate arms in white muslin sleeves were positioned upon the cloth, her hands folded over one another near her waist. Her dark hair was feathered over her shoulders. She had already been washed, yet a thin slash could be seen at her throat. As Taktu entered the room, the ladies bowed and backed away from the bed.

Stunned, Taktu stumbled to the bed. He knelt beside his wife and placed his hand over hers, weeping unabashedly. His son silently followed. Caspar stood in disbelief at the door.

Taktu and Vima remained motionless for several minutes. At last a senior servant, Lariska, came forward to speak. As she told the story, Taktu drifted into the drama. He knew Sarah all too well. Her final thoughts became his own as he imagined the scene.

"Don't leave," she had warned him. "I have a foreboding, something dark related to Vima's birthday. I don't know what it is."

Taktu had laughed. "We'll be back by then. Calm your fears, my warrior."

"Master, eight men took us by surprise," Lariska explained. "They were special Huns, armed with daggers and swords. Our men fought well, but the few who had not rushed to the fire were overcome."

Taktu's imagination sped forward. *"A Kushan queen, by herself? What a coincidence," the Hun leader commented boldly as he walked behind the advance fighters into the queen's bedchamber.*

"You will not escape my husband and his men," Sarah replied as her hand slid under the pillow.

"We know about the king. He is precisely where he should be. No doubt lying on the battlefield outside the town. That

leaves us to do as we will with you."

A glint of silver quivered as Sarah flung her knife with astounding accuracy into the Hun leader's throat. "Appakke Nakte, have mercy," she whispered, "and protect Taktu, Vima, and our people."

Lariska continued. "The queen herself fought bravely, grabbing a dagger from under the pillow. Her throw was accurate and one of the attackers fell. She was very weak because the night before she had gone into birthing pains with her child, who came into the world early in the morning."

Taktu was not allowed in the room when Vima was born. But he relived the sounds of her pain and his fear when all was silent. It was Lariska who at last invited him in to see his wife and their first son.

"I think the Huns were not aware a baby had been born to her," the servant went on. "I hid with the newborn behind the doorway, praying for help and for the infant to remain invisible to their eyes. I would have given my life to save our queen, but what could I do other than protect the royal baby?

"Zhu Li stood before the queen and fought to the end. The Huns shouted at him like they hated him more than anyone . . . perhaps because of his Oriental blood. Even he was overcome at last, bound, and taken outside."

The scene reared again in Taktu's mind.

Their leader fallen, fighters tore the queen from her bed.

Zhu Li charged hopelessly into the room, slashing and stabbing his way between Sarah and the intruders.

"Zhu! Watch behind," Sarah shouted as more Huns poured into the room.

"Traitor!" the attackers spat at Zhu. "Worthless dog. You have left your Motherland to grovel for barbarians." Four men grabbed and held Zhu, whose calm demeanor aggravated the attackers as much as the injuries he had inflicted.

"I serve only One," Zhu replied, "as do the people I abide with. Leave us in peace." His words were met with raucous ridicule.

"And then . . . ," Lariska broke down completely into sobs, "they murdered our queen."

Taktu envisioned the Hun knife ruthlessly cutting through the air to meet the soft throat of his wife. "Taktu, I love . . . " he heard her say.

"As she fell, more of our guards came in and there was a great commotion. At last our men defeated them, but it was too late."

Behind Caspar came another cry, the wail of a newborn. A nursemaid entered the room. As she carried the tightly swaddled baby, she bowed before the king and prince. Taktu did not resist as she gently placed the bundle in his arms.

"Your daughter, the royal princess," Lariska said.

5

THE WAY TO SHAMBALLA

In the mountains outside Kapisa

THE YOUNG PRINCE AND HIS FATHER TRUDGED UP A narrow mountain trail, accompanied by Caspar. This evening's event could not be postponed, even with the deaths of Sarah and of Zhu Li, whose surviving son was also in the party. The members of the Order expected a messenger and the meeting included a ritual for Vima's tenth birthday. The king's advisor, Wenta, his wife, and their daughter Sanum were already up the mountain. Torch lights flickered at the entrance to a cave.

The four, somber and exhausted, climbed the trail without conversation. Zhu signaled their approach to the others with the sound of an owl, as his father had taught him. Years ago the elder Zhu had communicated this way with the small band retrieving their horses from the Hun encampment. The hooting cry made Taktu shudder at the loss of his friend, sadness eclipsed only by the loss of his wife.

He thought back to when he was seventeen and full of pride in the accomplishments of his people. His great-grandfather's kingdom lay in an Asian valley called the Tarim Basin. The nomadic people were Tokhars, whom the Chinese called Yueh-chih.

Taktu's father, Kajula Kadphises, united the tribes of the Yueh-chih. Once united, they became known as Kushans. Their empire grew.

The Kushans passed both skills and legends from generation to generation. One legend was of Shamballa, where, it was said, a great soul, the Ancient of Days, came from heaven with thousands of companions bearing the light of God in their hearts.

Storytellers elaborated that the people of the world were mired in ignorance and darkness when the Divine Hero and his band came to teach humankind.

But, as years went by, progeny of this holy retinue were absorbed among the people of the world and they forgot their divine origins. The Ancient of Days withdrew to heaven and the beautiful city disappeared.

After many years, other holy luminaries—avatars— came forward to awaken and enlighten men and women. Taktu knew the five-hundred-year-old saga of Siddhartha, who became a great Buddha. During his travels to India, Taktu learned of Krishna, and while a boy in Persia, the priests told him of Zoroaster. Melchizedek was another legendary teacher and priest.

Members of the far-flung Order knew only a few of their counterparts. Communication between them could take months or years. Often contact was completely lost. Yet, they managed to hold a common belief: Prepare for the coming of another great avatar, prophesied to be the Savior. They did not know exactly what that meant or how it would happen, but they knew it was pivotal for the progress of human-kind. They knew this Savior would show all people the way back to their innate holiness, symbolized to the Kushans by Shamballa.

WOVEN INTO THIS FABRIC OF TAKTU'S LIFE WAS SARAH. He remembered their meeting when he and his father, King Kajula, arrived in Kabul with a few of their men and pitched colorful tents outside the city.

For many months before the trip, Kajula's priests and advisors in Kapisa prepared for marital negotiations. They sent emissaries to Kabul, prayed and calculated astrology. Initial greetings with Sarah's family were not deemed posi-tive, however, as the bride in question was nowhere to be found. Embarrassed, the royal family delayed negotiations. It wasn't until after midnight that she was found in her bed, lamenting that she was ill.

Growing up in Magdala, a city on the Sea of Galilee,

Sarah was descended from royalty. Her parents gave her the name and title of Sarah—princess—and considered her lineage sacred. When she became a young woman, they placed around her neck a gold chain with a medallion—the Signet.

Sarah was sixteen when her family, seeking freedom from Caesar's reach and a place to live peacefully, left Magdala. They followed the trade routes toward Asia. They pushed eastward, finally settling in Kabul.

The morning after Sarah claimed to be sick, she wrapped her veil about her and commanded a workman to saddle her horse. The sun was rising over the mountains, and Sarah planned to ride out across the flatlands before others had time to complain that this was not the proper pastime for a princess, especially since negotiations were in progress regarding her marriage.

Sarah rode swiftly onto the plain, noting the visitors' tents in the distance. "These people," she thought, "are so strange. Their skins are whiter than a goat's. They speak differently. I understand their Aramaic, but their other tongue is far from me. Their homeland is a long journey from here. I will never see my family again.

"Heavenly Father," she called out plaintively to the sky as she rode, "what is your will for me?"

Neither was Taktu, only seventeen, very willing for an encounter with a bride, especially one who could not be found. He assured his father that there was plenty of time and plenty of tribes with princesses. Taktu was ready to strike camp and return home. His father, however, was unrelenting and retreated to his tent for prayer and consultation with his advisors.

With the early morning light, Taktu slipped out of his tent, took his falcon on his arm, and mounted his horse to ride along the river. His red hair shone redder in the early rays of the sun, and his young beard sprouted in a neat, thin patch over his chin. He hunched his head down into the hood of his cloak to shield himself from the mountain breeze biting into his skin.

His mare picked her way through the sand and rocks. Stark, jagged mountains rose abruptly in the distance on the opposite side of the river. There was little shrubbery. The entire scene turned roseate as the light climbed the mountains.

Around a bluff, Taktu stopped and uncapped the falcon. Letting her fly off from the leather on his arm, he watched the bird soar in wider circles, higher and higher. Suddenly she dropped like lightning from the sky. As the bird screeched and swooped to the ground, Taktu noticed a rider galloping in his direction along the river.

The rider stopped and looked at Taktu. The falcon stood between them on top of her prey, a brown hare under her talons.

"Strange," Taktu thought. "Why is a woman riding by

herself this early?" He raised his hand and gently called out, "Peace," in Aramaic.

Sarah was wary. She sat tensely, prepared to outrace the intruder along the twisting path she knew so well back to her home.

Nevertheless, as she watched the slow approach of the fair-skinned young man with shining red hair, Sarah felt the disconcerting sensation that she was watching *herself.* "What does this mean?" she questioned. "Why does this stranger seem like *part of me?*" It was an odd perception—something she had never imagined and that she had certainly never experienced. It was not unpleasant or frightening; instead, she felt familiarity and kinship.

As Taktu rode closer, he noticed that the woman's clothing was in the style of the West: long, woolen robes and a veil over her head. Her coloring was more olive and brown than that of his people, and wavy brown hair flowed over her shoulders. He saw her face peering toward him, and even at a distance noticed the penetrating brown eyes.

But, in an instant, the beautiful face he watched blurred and turned into his own face. Startled, Taktu squinted hard and, turning his horse toward the falcon, dismounted, letting the reins fall over his horse's head.

Kneeling, Taktu nudged the falcon onto his arm, cut a chunk of meat and fed it to the bird before placing the leather hood back over the falcon's head. With a naturalness that was totally foreign to him, especially with women, he said, "It would be my honor if you would join me for breakfast, that is, if you like roasted rabbit." He smiled.

In a surreal flow he watched Sarah dismount and gather dried grass and sticks to start a fire. Taktu quickly prepared the rabbit. Sarah and Taktu sat on the river bank, laughing and working in tandem to prepare their simple meal.

Their wedding was successfully finalized. Sarah returned with Taktu to Kapisa.

But today, after only fourteen years, Sarah was gone. It was unbearable to continue without her. Sarah was as much a part of the king as his heart or his head was. Through the Order, they shared a passion for the sacredness of Appakke Nakte in their lives, and they longed to unite humankind in their young, idealistic dreams of brotherhood.

Ten years earlier to the day, Sarah bore a son, Vima, of whom Taktu was very proud. And now he had an infant daughter, who, he feared, would always remind him of his anguish and guilt at the loss of his wife. His former dreams seemed pointless. In shock and grief, Taktu fell impenetrably sullen.

AT THE ENTRANCE TO THE CAVE, SANUM GREETED THEM, a torch in hand. She bowed her head to Taktu and Vima. "We are deeply grieved by your great loss, which is also ours." She turned to Zhu. "And we will never forget your heroic father. I feel the queen and Zhu Li are with us now. Come, all is ready."

They bent low to pass under a small archway and turn a corner, feeling the ceiling with their hands. The passageway opened into a small room, where the space above them was lost in darkness extending beyond the torchlight and campfire. Cushions for each of them had been placed around the fire, and one extra cushion completed the circle. At each place was a small jade bowl.

Seated, Wenta and his wife smiled warmly. They were fulfilling their roles as the priest and priestess of the ceremony.

"Our Father bless you and send you great comfort," Wenta said. "Please be comfortable. We will begin. Our unknown guest will soon arrive with instructions."

Together the pair chanted an Om, the universal sound, joined by the others until it reverberated through the cave. As each felt the resonance and became focused on his or her heart, Wenta sang an ancient hymn.

Appakke Nakte,
We know you in the secret chamber
Where you have placed the fire.

The others sang in response:

We keep your flame
In the secret chamber of our hearts.

Nodding in rhythm to his chant, Wenta continued:

We praise your light
That does all mighty works on earth.
We praise your flame burning brightly
In each one.

The others responded:

We keep your flame
In the secret chamber of our hearts.

The hymn went on:

Mighty are the works of the Father, I AM,
   sapphire flame
From whence comes our power.
Mighty are the works of the Spirit, I AM,
   rose ruby flame
From whence comes our love.
Mighty are the works of the Son, I AM,
   yellow topaz flame

From whence comes our wisdom.
These three cradled in the white fire
of the Mother, I AM.

The group responded:

We keep your flame for all life
In the secret lotus of our hearts.

"We are ready," Wenta said. "Vima Kadphises, remove your tunic and come forward." Sanum brought her father a small wooden box with dyes and an ivory awl, carved so finely that it could delicately pierce the skin to leave the dye behind in a tattoo. She placed the unused cushion between her father and the fire. There, Vima stretched out on his back. The wound in his side was swollen and red, showing through a layer of Zhu's paste that had hardened over it. And, although he was a hero, his chest was white and youthful because he was but a boy.

The king's advisor dipped his awl in the dye and placed it just to the left of the boy's heart. As the others continued their hymns, Wenta worked meticulously to tattoo a six-pointed star, less than the size of a small coin in diameter, and in the center he drew the three tiny entwined flames on a circular base. These he colored with blue, yellow, and rose dyes.

As he worked he explained, "This is the true size of the seed flames of Appakke Nakte within you. Water them with your devotion and the right use of the love, wisdom, and power of our Father, and they will grow on the light of the Mother at their base. By this sign, know that you will be the next king of the Kushans."

All continued to sing and chant their praise of the flame of life until Vima at last returned to his place and they fell silent.

Then Zhu broke the quiet as he softly sang a mantra in his native tongue. All bowed their heads, recognizing his song to the Heavenly Mother of his lands. His father had often called to her for mercy. Zhu's invocation was offered for the souls of their lost family members. When he ended with an Om, the others joined him.

As the Om faded, they saw someone standing in the shadows outside their circle. He was smiling, with his right hand raised in a sign of peace and blessing.

Taktu immediately recognized the same shepherd who had come thirteen years ago with a secret message confirming the arrival of the avatar. Never could the king forget that figure. He moved to stand, but the shepherd gestured to sit and said, "Peace to you all."

The guest took the empty cushion by the fire and looked penetratingly at each of them.

"Sons and daughters, my message is simple, for the hour has come when the son of God you await must be prepared for his mission."

Turning to Taktu he continued, "Meet him in six months in Sind."

Taktu understood that the shepherd was not only the messenger he had met years ago, but a holy man and a secret member of the Order. He responded respectfully, as he had been trained to do since childhood.

"How will I know him, Master?" he asked.

"You will know him as you know me—by an inner recognition."

Facing Caspar he commented, "My son, you have done your job well. Continue to stay alert to instructions from the Order."

Turning back toward the fire, the shepherd said, "The Father's peace and blessings to all of you." From a leather pouch at his side, he took a flat bread and broke it into pieces, giving a portion to each of them. "Divine Mother," he said, "bless this bread with your light, that we, your sons and daughters made of clay and fire, may be one with you now."

As they took the bread and ate it, the shepherd took the flask and poured wine into the jade bowls they passed to him and then returned around the circle.

"Heavenly Father," he said, "let this be the light of your being coursing through us, uniting us with you and the light of all humankind. Prepare us for the Savior who makes all things new."

As they meditated, the guest rose. Extending his palm

over them as a sign of blessing, he said, "Remember, all is for your testing. Be ever grateful, my children, to our Father and Mother of Lights." He turned and left.

The cave, though still lit by the fire, did not seem as bright. Taktu moved into the shadows, retreating from the circle and from the light of the fire. Even though he comprehended the holiness of the ceremony, his despair gripped him and he sat, unapproachable, in the dark.

The others looked into the fire, feeling their lives inexplicably altered.

Vima felt older, as though he could never be a child again. His chest marking smarted, and he felt dizzy and nauseated from exhaustion and the throbbing wound at his side. He lay down with his head on his cushion, and thought of the shepherd, experiencing again the warmth of his presence.

Vima placed his hand over the wound at his side and imagined the shepherd's hand placed over his own. He saw the shepherd smile at him, and, amazingly, a warm, comforting, tingling sensation came through his hand and he felt the pain lessen and disappear.

Sighing in relief and fatigue, his mind flitted and he thought of his father sitting by himself in the shadows.

Vima wanted more than anything to feel his father's hand on his shoulder and to shout their grief together to the heavens. But the boy would not cry. Though the evening's events were auspicious, he was acutely aware of a piercing aloneness unlike anything he had ever known before. As his head cleared from the throbbing and swirling images of the day, Vima struggled with another pain, an ache around his heart.

Today he was honored as a hero and marked as the future king. And now he grieved the loss of his mother—and of his isolated father.

JESUS' JOURNEY TO THE EAST

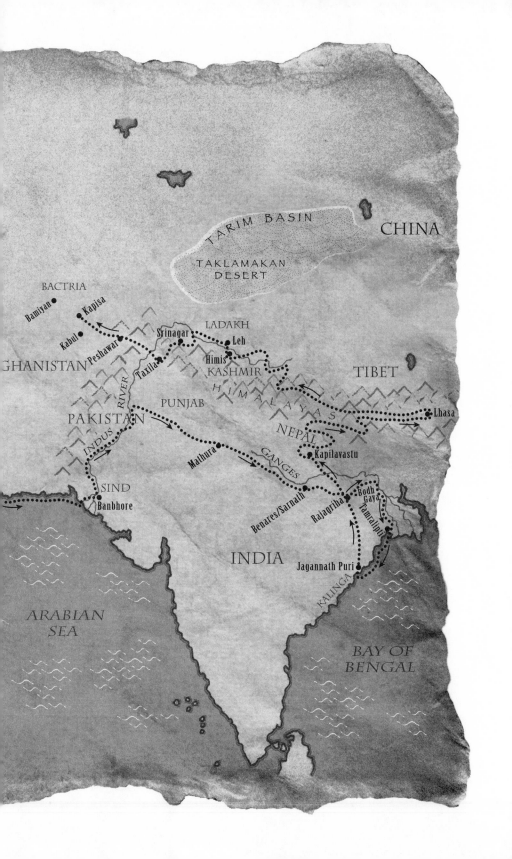

CHINA

TARIM BASIN

TAKLAMAKAN
DESERT

BACTRIA

Bamiyan

Kapisa

Kabul

LADAKH

Srinagar

Leh

Peshawar

GHANISTAN

Taxila

Himis

KASHMIR

TIBET

HIMALAYAS

PUNJAB

Lhasa

PAKISTAN

NEPAL

INDUS RIVER

Mathura

Kapilavastu

GANGES

SIND

Banbhore

Benares/Sarnath

Bodh Gaya

Rajagriha

Tamralipti

INDIA

Jagannath Puri

ARABIAN
SEA

KALINGA

BAY OF
BENGAL

6

THE HIDDEN TEACHER

Six months later, in India

JESUS STARTED FROM HIS SLEEP AND SAT UP ON HIS MAT.
He was bathed in sweat. The movement woke Joseph of
Arimathea.

"What is it? Another nightmare?"

Jesus nodded.

"Tell me."

Their ship rocked gently on the quiet Arabian Sea. At
night they rested in the space Joseph had procured in the cool
open air near their cargo on deck. Awa lay nearby. At the
sound of Joseph's voice, their helper inquired, "Everything all
right, Master?"

Hanuman scampered over the top of some sacks and
perched authoritatively on Jesus' lap, making them all laugh.
Joseph motioned for Awa to sit with them. The sun rose,
casting a faint light onto their circle. The crew continued
their toil toward Banbhore, at the mouth of the Indus River

in the Indian region of Sind. This morning, after many wearying days of travel, they would arrive at port.

Jesus looked at his uncle. "All I could see was the face of a Roman soldier glaring at me. He said, 'You'll never be a king!' and tried to grab me. Then I woke up." Jesus rubbed his face. "I don't know what it means."

Joseph was accustomed to the young man tossing in the night. Each nightmare was different. One had a threatening demon. Another time, Jesus challenged a teacher who then called for his arrest. Once, a woman approached him and spat out, "Give up now. You will fail." She laughed and disappeared from his dream.

Joseph recited a prayer to the angel Michael. He knew Jesus needed protection. Whatever the sons and daughters of the Creator did to advance light and understanding among men and women was often opposed by forces of darkness. Only devotion, determination, and the grace of the Almighty carried them through the setbacks.

"There are not as many Romans in this land," he said. "I doubt they will notice you here. Nevertheless, we'll stop calling you Jesus. Let's use the name Awa gave you—Issa."

"Yes, Master," Awa said, beaming. "Issa. It is a good name. Hanuman and I will guard you well." Awa stood up and gave a little bow. Hanuman jumped to his shoulder. "I will make the morning tea."

Jesus felt weak. He was damp with sweat after the

nightmare. Although relieved that the Roman soldier existed only in his dream, he would not allow himself to discount the message. Instead, he prayed to understand its significance. He asked his Father to give him peace.

Jesus strained to unravel why the Roman soldier said he would never be a king. "Am I to be a king?" Jesus silently asked his Father. He tried to brush the idea aside, but it would not leave. He could not see how the message of this nightmare fit into his life. All it could mean was trouble. He sensed danger and hardship for himself and his family. As the ship drew closer to the port and sounds and aromas drifted across the water, Jesus wondered, as he did after every nightmare, if he had made the right decision to travel with his uncle. No. He must follow the inner direction he felt so strongly. Once again, the young man collected himself and the tension eased as he resolved, "Father, not my will but thine be done."

"This is not Jerusalem," Joseph commented as he thought of the family's annual trips to the temple. "Better prepare yourself. Let's have a look." He grunted as he pushed up from the deck. Together, he and Jesus walked to the railing.

In the port they saw dozens of ships anchored closely together. Jesus had never seen so many colorful standards and oddly constructed vessels. Joseph explained that the bay was packed with traders from Greece, Rome, China, Africa, Persia, Arabia, the Mediterranean, and the faraway northern islands.

Approaching the land, they heard a cacophony of selling and bartering from the marketplace on shore. The pungent smell of people, animals, and spices permeated the air.

Joseph rested against the railing as he took in the sights
and sounds. He thought that he would never grow accustomed to the smells of this country. "This is our first stop.
We'll take a barge up the delta to Minnegarha. It's much
better for traders like us because land routes also cross there."

THEY REACHED BUSTLING MINNEGARHA ON THE SIXTH
day. The air was hot and sultry. Awa prepared the way for
his two masters and for the men who followed with the cargo
of wrapped bundles piled on their heads and backs. With
Hanuman on his shoulder, Awa scurried ahead into the
throng of people going about their daily lives. Bowing def-
erentially to the upper castes as he went along, he shouted
to the laborers, "Make way! Make way, now." Hanuman
screeched to add emphasis.

At first, some of the crowd looked askance or shot slurs
at the small man whose station deserved little or no attention. But when they saw the imposing, colorfully robed figure
of Joseph behind him, accompanied by an unusual foreign
young man dressed unpretentiously in white robe and brown
leather sandals, they parted and stared. Joseph was accustomed to this reaction, but Jesus found the masses over-

whelming. He had never seen such pressing humanity, nor had he ever heard the din of street life at such a roaring feverish pitch.

The travelers approached the central marketplace. Smells wafted up from little fires along both sides of the road, where people squatted and roasted nuts and flat breads or stirred their soups. A cow with red-tasseled horns roamed the lane. Shouts and arguments intensified as vendors hawked their wares.

"Master," Awa said, "I know of an inn on the other side of the marketplace."

The trio penetrated farther into the rows of stalls. Finally, they emerged at the center, which was dominated by a white tiered structure, circular at the bottom and rising in smaller concentric rings until it ended in a short spire at the top. A line of chanting people walked slowly in a circle around the base. Some people cast themselves flat on the ground after each step.

"A stupa," Joseph explained to his nephew. "This one may contain a relic of the Buddha or a sacred text."

Jesus paused to watch the men and women in their simple practice of prayer. "What do they ask for?" he wondered out loud.

"I'm told they pray for the benefit of the world and to be born into a good family in their next life."

They walked on. Outside the ring of circling devotees,

the most destitute held up their bowls. The blind, the diseased, and nursing mothers pleaded for alms. Thin, dirty children also extended their hands. Many, both young and old, were severely deformed.

A man with no arms and whose legs ended above the knees thrust his dirty, rag-covered torso directly in front of Jesus. The beggar gripped a basket with his teeth. Seeing him, Awa stopped and excitedly acted as if he would strike the man. "Get back!" he said. "Make way and do not disturb the master."

Jesus said, "Uncle Joseph brought me with him to study more about the Buddha. Isn't it true that he taught compassion?" Joseph produced a few copper coins and placed them in the basket. The recipient grinned, quickly bent his torso, and dropped the basket to his lap. He picked up the coins with his mouth and let them fall into a shabby pouch hanging from his neck. Then he gave a loud prayer of blessing.

Awa was exasperated. "I am not a Buddhist. If you give to these untouchables, they will only cry for more!"

Jesus said nothing. Awa suddenly understood the hypocrisy of his angry words. He dropped his head, ashamed that he had disappointed his master.

Jesus asked, "Do you have any refreshments, Awa?"

Awa fumbled in his pouch and produced a pomegranate. Jesus broke it open. Kneeling down, he cradled the surprised man in one arm while feeding him fruit with the other hand. Red juice rolled down the beggar's chin. Jesus wiped it with his sleeve. The man's eyes widened and his body trembled with shock, fear, and disbelief. He tried to smile, but his chin quivered, and he burst into tears at this unexpected tenderness.

"All are God's children," Jesus said. "Life is full of suffering. Yet there is a way to overcome. We don't know the purpose behind this one's tragedy."

Awa stared, visibly moved. Curious passersby gathered at the unusual scene. The supplicants stopped clamoring. A Brahman's face shifted from shock to disgust. A surprised young woman, with several children and a baby, stood watching the scene.

The overlord of the beggars, angrily brandishing a thick leather strap, strode into the midst of the group. His job was to be sure his people worked at gathering alms. "What's going on here?" he demanded in Sindhi, spreading his legs. The ring of onlookers quickly broke up. Awa realized that his masters could not understand what had been said. He stepped toward the overlord, bowing deeply. Hanuman ran to Joseph's feet. Looking at his own knees, Awa threw his arms out to each side and panted, "My lord, they do not understand."

The strap flew across his back, cutting the flesh. Still bowing, Awa continued, "They are from another land."

Jesus quickly rose and Joseph came forward, placing his

hands on Awa's arms. In Aramaic, he said to the overlord, "This man belongs to me. Let him be."

The overlord stared at Joseph blankly, understanding by action rather than language. He frowned and gestured with his arms for them to leave. He picked up his mendicant like a sack of rice. The overlord glared at Joseph one more time, then quickly turned and strode away with the beggar under his massive arm.

Jesus carefully poured water from his flask onto Awa's back and dressed it with healing herbs from his pouch; his mother had crushed the herbs and made them into a salve.

"Thank you, Awa," Jesus said. "You were fearless and quick-thinking on our behalf."

Awa's face flushed. He knew he had done well. His actions came from an impulse that surprised him. He was at a loss for words.

Joseph was prepared to move his men forward when he noticed a tall man, with red hair and a red beard, seated on a magnificent white stallion. The impressive stranger was watching them from across the square. A young boy was with him. Mounted soldiers were stationed before and behind.

King Taktu looked intently at Jesus, Joseph, and Awa. Joseph returned the gaze, but was startled by a piercing war cry and a thundering company of hooded riders who roared into the market.

Bystanders screamed and retreated behind stalls and

against the walls of houses. The Kushan guards spun around and drew swords against the attack.

Joseph, Jesus, and Awa were spectators at the assassination. They saw spears fly and then the hooded party retreated the way they came. A group of Kushan guards split off and charged after them.

All who remained saw the boy, Vima, lifeless on the ground.

Taktu dropped down and buried his head in his son's chest. He lifted Vima and stood with him in his arms. The boy's head rolled back and his mouth gaped open. Vima's tunic was soaked in blood around his heart, and Taktu's pale white face was streaked with it. Stunned, he carried the body to the boy's horse and draped Vima facedown over the saddle, covering him with his own cloak. The king stood trembling. Speaking in Sindhi with a halting voice, he said simply, "Let there be thirty days of mourning for the prince."

The marketplace was silent. The king remounted and led his men out of sight.

Joseph, Jesus, and Awa were stunned. Awa translated the king's brief declaration.

Jesus leaned against a wall and slid down to his haunches. His calves and shoulders ached. The blood drained from his face and sweat ran down his back. He buried his head in his arms to combat the dizzy sickness enveloping him.

"This is where I have come to study?" he asked himself.

"My mother was right. The Father can teach me as well at home." Although criminal punishments in Jerusalem were horrendous, with frequent crucifixions by the Romans or stonings by the Hebrews, at least he knew the factions and the environment. Here, in just a few short days, Jesus had seen pain and poverty beyond description, false accusation, and a murder that took place before his eyes so swiftly it was incomprehensible. It was all too chaotic.

Joseph was also appalled. The tall man on the white horse had caught his eye. There was an undeniable connection. The much-experienced merchant could not make sense of what had happened or the feelings. Fear, grief, awe, and confusion mixed together and he hardly knew what to do next.

Awa was anxious to leave the scene in case there was more violence to come. "Master, let's go," he ventured. Finally the travelers made their way through the frantic crowd.

AT THE INN, AWA UNROLLED HIS MASTERS' MATS ONTO wooden beds in their quarters. The afternoon sun streamed through three windows, small and high in the wall to prevent unwanted visitors.

After the dramatic events of the day, they were all surprised when a messenger arrived. Addressing Awa at the door, he said, "The king would like to see your masters." Then, observing the two just beyond Awa, he spoke in Aramaic: "The king seeks the pleasure of your company. Can you come with me now?" He bowed courteously.

"Who will guard the masters' supplies?" Awa objected. "I must go everywhere with my masters. They are not accustomed to this land, and they cannot leave their goods unprotected."

"I will station men," the messenger replied.

Awa eyed him suspiciously, but Joseph interceded and said, "We will come with you."

After placing shawls over their heads in respect for Taktu's declaration of mourning, Joseph and Jesus, accompanied by Awa with Hanuman, followed the messenger through town until they came to the city walls. Just outside were large white tents, decorated with dark appliqué symbols and glowing from the cast of the sun. Soldiers patrolled.

At the largest tent, the guide explained to men at the entrance that the guests had arrived. Jesus, Joseph, and Awa were ushered in. Hanuman sat on the back of Awa's neck, his tiny arms wrapped around Awa's forehead like a headband. The three paused inside the opening and took in the scene.

A Persian rug lay across the grass, filling the space with rich ruby, blue, and gold colors. Large cushions were piled around each side of the tent. Directly in front of the visitors was a long, low table spread with food and intricately painted clay bowls.

On the other side of the table sat King Taktu in a relaxed pose. He wore a clean tunic, and though washed, his face remained serious and he looked fatigued.

Standing next to him was another impressive figure. Smiling, the man wore Hun armor and held a black hood crumpled in his hand. His long spear leaned against the cloth wall of the tent.

A girl, younger than Jesus, sat at one end of the table playing a stringed instrument. An older gentleman sat behind her.

At the other end of the table was the most startling sight of all. Young prince Vima sat smiling, his bloody shirt open, revealing his perfectly unharmed chest, a broken bladder skin of blood still hanging over his heart. The room filled with fragrance as a manservant came with a fresh tunic and a basin of steaming herb-filled water to wash the prince.

Sitting by Vima was a lean young man with dark, straight hair. He was dressed in Hun military attire.

Joseph bowed in the direction of the king and said, "My lord, I am Joseph of Arimathea, a merchant. My land, my people, and my home are far to the west. This is my great-nephew, Issa, and my servant, Awa. We have been traveling many months on a trading journey. We are honored to be in your presence." He bowed again. "And, if I may say so, we are curious about your kind invitation, especially after seeing a great deal of excitement in the marketplace today."

The man with the flashing smile standing next to the

king laughed heartily. Acknowledging their bewilderment, he replied, "I am Caspar, a king from Persia, and a fearsome Hun with a deadly spear. I'm quite an actor, too." He bowed. "This is my old friend, Taktu, ruler of the Kushans. And that young warrior"—he cocked his head toward Vima—"is his son and heir, Prince Vima Kadphises, whose life, along with the king's, is the most highly desired prize of our enemy.

"But let us have dinner now," he continued. "I return to my land in the morning and tonight we must commemorate Vima's last day for many years as a prince."

The guests were still baffled and unsettled. Why, they wondered, would this be the boy's last day as a prince? And why were they invited to commemorate it?

They all took places on cushions around the low table, with the exception of Awa and Hanuman, who sat slightly behind Joseph, on the carpet. Awa ran his hand over the luxurious rug and reached across the table for grapes, which he fed to himself and his small companion.

"Issa," Caspar continued, "where are you from and what brings you to Minnegarha?" At the table, servants poured tea and pomegranate juice and placed sweetmeats into each bowl.

"I am from Nazareth. My father and mother settled there from Egypt."

"You were born in Egypt, then?" Caspar eyed him quizzically.

"No, sir, I was born in Bethlehem, but my parents moved to Egypt when I was a baby. I don't remember it. And, my great-uncle brings me on his trips from time to time so that I can learn more of the world."

"I see. And what is it you would like to learn of the world?" Caspar pressed.

Jesus looked at his great-uncle, who said, "The boy is very tired after a long journey, my lord. Allow me to answer for him. I bring my great-nephew on my trips to broaden his education. Perhaps one day he will be a valuable assistant to me."

"Yes, I understand," said Caspar. "I was once in Bethlehem myself to see a baby. His mother and father called him Jesus. Herod went to tragic extremes to be rid of him. I don't believe Herod was successful, which would mean that this Jesus and our Vima here have much in common. One was once hunted and despised by the Roman authorities, and one is now hunted and despised by the Huns. Both have much to learn to complete their missions for our Father."

Taktu's silence and grim face created a somber atmosphere. Caspar turned to him.

"Tonight, Taktu, put away some of your mourning. We have much to celebrate."

Taktu's face did not lighten.

Turning back to the guests, Caspar continued, "My friend lost his queen to the Huns six months ago. Since then, he hardly speaks. He only thinks of protecting his son and his kingdom."

"Enough talk!" Taktu said gruffly. "My son must not be recognized in this kingdom again for many years. I am losing him, too. I only hope the scene today, which Caspar devised and I reluctantly agreed to, will convince everyone that Vima is no longer a target. I am determined to establish a great empire for my son to rule one day."

Speaking directly to Jesus, the king added, "I saw you in the town today. I have been sent to the region of Sind to meet the Savior." Stern and impatient, he continued, with his gaze upon the young man. "I believe I have accomplished the directive. If you explain what this means and whether I have recognized the Savior, I will return to my lands in the North."

Jesus looked back at Taktu. He didn't understand what it meant to be a "savior." The drama lay hidden, waiting for the ordained moment to be revealed. His words came spontaneously. "I am his son and I have come to do the Father's will."

Taktu sighed and wiped a hand over his face. "We who are gathered with you here are all of the Order of Melchizedek." The king took the gold Signet from beneath his tunic.

Jesus was surprised. He noticed that Taktu's medallion was essentially the same as the one worn by his mother. Perhaps hers had been crafted in finer detail. Many times his mother and father recounted the story of the star that had appeared and the coming of kings and shepherds—some who were members of the Order—to see him as their long-awaited emissary from heaven.

Taktu continued, "But one son of God is the Savior. My warriors are ready to guard him and Vima as they travel to pursue their training."

Jesus wondered what to answer. He didn't think of himself as a savior. He only knew his Father had a plan for him that the young man was determined to fulfill, and that whatever it was gave him nightmares. He asked for inner direction.

Jesus relaxed as he abandoned himself to the will of the Almighty. A surge of the Father's love poured through him and toward the pain solidified around Taktu's heart. How much love and how many years would it take to melt such pain?

Jesus' voice was calm and sure. "I am he you seek. People say I have been born in answer to prophecy. Some say I am to be a savior. I only know I am here to do my Father's will."

All were silent, weighing in their hearts this confirmation.

Jesus felt relief. He had taken a step into his Father's arms. There was no return. He continued, "I have come to find my teacher, who will instruct me in mysteries I will need for my Father's work."

Taktu leaned back on his elbow. "And who is your teacher? Where is this one to be found?"

"That I do not know," Jesus replied.

Suddenly Awa brightened. "Yes, Master. It is not difficult. It is our custom, even for the most holy men in my land, to seek a personal guide, a guru. That is our way of saying 'teacher.' Yes, yes. I can take you to all the holy men who instruct the Brahmans and the Kshatriyas. You can pick the one for you. And for the son of the king, of course," he added excitedly.

As Awa spoke, Jesus saw a small shrine set against the side of the tent. A wooden chest was covered with a purple silk cloth. On it were three brass bowls: one filled with grain, one with water, and another with fruit. An oil lamp burned before two small carved stone figures. One sat cross-legged, meditating, with a serene smile on his face. The other figure stood with the right hand raised and a circular halo carved around the head.

The altar gripped Jesus' attention. His face turned questioning. He replied to Awa, "My teacher is not among those that you mention. My teacher is one of these." He pointed toward the shrine.

Zhu, who played the role of a Hun assassin in the staged drama earlier that day, moved to the chest. He carefully picked up the seated figure and brought it closer to the table. "Lord Gautama Buddha," he said, "came to bring light to the world. He was born in this land as a prince, Siddhartha, but when he learned of people outside the palace suffering and dying, he gave up his kingdom and family to seek the antidote to pain. He tried the life of austerity, fasting and depriving himself of comfort. At last he realized that was not the way for many to escape suffering. Finally he meditated, letting all desires flee, and denying the temptations of Mara, the evil one, until he became one with all of life and found enlightenment as the key to happiness. Is Buddha your teacher?"

Jesus contemplated the figure. He had heard of Buddha from his great uncle, who insisted that Jesus come to this land to understand the teachings of Gautama. Joseph also wanted Jesus to delve into the stories of Krishna from the ancient texts in order to decipher the young man's possible future role in Palestine.

His uncle's cursory descriptions of Buddhism and Hinduism were compelling. Jesus readily identified with Gautama Buddha's care for every part of life and renunciation of material wealth and other worldly desires. The concept of latent Buddha-potential in the poor as well as the rich made sense, though it was hard to reconcile in this strange society of caste systems or in the context of his home, where slavery juxtaposed with privileged classes. Siddhartha had set aside his wealthy status and disregarded castes. His way offered hope to the wretched. Jesus felt the same calling.

And yet, the figure of Gautama Buddha did not speak to him as a personal teacher to guide his life. He replied slowly and thoughtfully, "This one seems like a grandfather, as if

I knew him long ago." He turned his head back toward the shrine. "Who is that one?" he asked.

Zhu replaced the Buddha and brought forward the standing figure.

Taktu said, "Maitreya, the Coming Buddha. He will come to inaugurate a new time of peace and understanding. How can he be your teacher?"

Jesus asked himself the same question. "What does the Coming Buddha have to do with me? His image and his name seem so familiar. I already feel close to him." Jesus knew he had to find out more about Maitreya.

"I don't know," he replied, "but I must find him. He is the father of my spirit and the teacher I seek." His sudden affinity with Maitreya was strong.

No one understood how the shepherd entered the tent unannounced. But there the old man stood, as he had in the cave six months earlier and in the palace with a message for Taktu many years before that.

The shepherd laughed as he limped his way toward the table. "Maitreya is never far!"

Sanum set aside the stringed instrument she had been playing and brought a large cushion for the visitor. She held his bent arm and helped him sit, motioning servants to bring food.

The shepherd sighed. "You have done well, good king, to notice Issa in the crowd." He smiled warmly toward Taktu.

"And our friend, Caspar, has shown great wisdom with his plan to make people think the young prince, Vima, is dead. Thanks to him, it is safe for me to leave with the boys tomorrow and take them to Maitreya," he added.

They all stared at him in amazement. Awa's mouth dropped completely open before he blurted out, "Who are you? How can you possibly take them to Maitreya? Where will you go? How do you know where Maitreya is or if he is a person at all? Besides, my master can go nowhere without me. And he cannot leave his uncle, who has many months of trading to complete. It is out of the question."

The visitor was unperturbed. "I am called Maitreyajna, little Maitreya," the old man said. "I am a simple shepherd. And I will take you to Maitreya, on one condition." His face became stern and serious as he looked from Vima to Jesus— and then he motioned toward Zhu and included him in the group of boys. "You each must accept me as your guru, and obey me without question. You must be my servants. You can only be kings, statesmen, and holy men if you first prove that you are slaves—not *my* slaves, but the Father's slaves, as He works through me."

Turning to Awa, he continued, "And you can come, too, if you choose, and obey the same condition." Laughing he added, "Your monkey friend is also invited. Perhaps he will agree to the condition."

Awa's mouth flapped open and shut a few times. Only

the upper caste Brahmans and the Kshatriyas were allowed to study anything holy. His withered hand was already testimony to that. And *this* man, if he were real, was offering to take him along. "This must be a trick," Awa said huffily and without guile.

Maitreyajna laughed again. "You will be a great help, my son. Your mouth quickly brings out what most minds would like to keep hidden. No, I have no trick. The trickster is in your heads and will come to each of you tonight. Will you choose to be parted from the others and come with me, a stranger, or stay and continue your search on your own? If you choose to come with me, you must know that the journey to Maitreya will take many years. We will go fearlessly on our own, without guards or weapons.

"You have until midday tomorrow to decide. If you come, dress simply, as a traveler, and bring only a pouch and a staff like mine if you like. I will join you at the well next to this road on the other side of the first hill. Now I will go to my place of rest."

Sanum jumped up to help the shepherd rise. The old man left the table without touching the sweetmeats. Noticing, she quickly picked up the bowl and, bowing slightly, presented it to him with both hands. "Here, take these," she said. "Surely the food will satisfy your hunger and the bowl will be useful on your travels." As she stood before Maitreyajna, she felt he was asking her a question.

The old shepherd took the bowl and smiled. "Thank you, my child," he said, before he limped out of the tent.

"Be careful," Awa cautioned the others. "There are many charlatans in this land."

7

NEW ROADS

Outside Minnegarha, the following day

IT WAS HOT AND HUMID AT MIDDAY. PEOPLE OF THE SMALL village gathered at the well for water.

Joseph of Arimathea, in his colorful foreign garments, stood out from the crowd. He sat on a rock in the shade of a flowering tree. On the ground, a layer of dropped lavender-colored blossoms surrounded him. He fanned his face with a small palm branch and controlled his emotions about his nephew's decision to follow the unusual shepherd.

Joseph was convinced it was a good choice, but he had not anticipated their sudden separation and was forced to completely trust the Heavenly Father with Jesus' care. He recalled the dinner with Mary and Joseph before they departed from Nazareth. He marveled, in retrospect, at Mary's brave separation from her son.

To ease his concern, Joseph insisted that Awa go along, and he gave Jesus a sum of money to start their journey.

Perhaps these steps would help him explain to Mary why he let her boy join the group.

Jesus sat on the edge of the well, watching for Maitreyajna, while Awa filled a water bag. Once again Jesus would be separated from Joseph and all family connection. There was an emptiness in his gut that made him continue to question his decision to travel with Maitreyajna. "How am I to know this is the path you intend for me, Father?" he implored. Shouldn't divine direction be more clear? His emotions swung back and forth between doubt and certainty, anxiousness and determination. It was not whether he wanted to fulfill the Almighty's plan that he questioned. Of that Jesus was certain. But was he making the right choice to accompany Maitreyajna?

Joseph sensed his nephew's turmoil. "Sometimes the Father's will calls us to leave behind the familiar and step into the unknown, walking in faith," he said. "Always take the next practical step and you will find the Father's will."

Zhu came swiftly up the road. The young Chinese man was dressed in a simple brown tunic and trousers. He sat down quietly next to Jesus.

Joseph rose as he saw a man and a woman approach. The woman carried a baby in her arms. A boy walked close behind. When the group was near, Joseph recognized the king, Taktu, and his son, but did not recall the female with them.

Taktu strode up to Joseph. The ruler looked even more

pained than he had the night before.

"My son, Vima, is ready to go with Maitreyajna," Taktu said coldly.

Without turning, he referred to the woman. "This is a nursemaid, and the baby she holds is my daughter. I have not named the child. The nursemaid calls her Little Princess." His eyes narrowed and he continued hastily, "As I have said, I must concentrate on the stability of my kingdom."

Taktu paused and pulled his shoulders back. "I request that you take this child and her nursemaid back to her mother's homeland. My wife's people are from the West, as you are. She often spoke of her sister's household in Magdala and received messages from traders that her sister and family were happy and successful. Can you find them? Perhaps Magdala is not far from your home. I will provide all that is needed for their journey and pay for your trouble."

Joseph shuddered at the thought of the man's grief. "The money is not a concern, but she belongs here with you," he said.

Jesus and Zhu joined the king and Joseph. Jesus looked intently at the crying baby.

Taktu became agitated. "We must not take long. We are drawing too much attention to my son. Go, Vima. Sit under the trees where you will not be noticed."

The boy reluctantly obeyed. The burning lump in his throat and the loneliness he felt were unbearable. He wanted to shake his father and say, "Stop! I saved you once, but you are *dead*. You are crazy. Your grief has made you a madman. You are my father. Don't send me *and* my sister away. Is this what my mother would have wanted?" As he sat apart under the trees, Vima flushed with shame that these things would not come from his lips.

Jesus took the baby from the nursemaid's arms. He held her against his chest and patted her back. There was something special about this infant. She seemed familiar. At once the tiny girl stopped crying, sat up in his arms, and smiled. "Uncle, can you take her? I think her rank as princess is dangerous here, and her father is burdened by his grief. In Magdala, her mother's people will teach her our belief in the Almighty."

Joseph sighed. His small and changing company had received many surprises in the last twenty-four hours. "All right," he said at last.

"We should call her Mary in honor of my mother," Jesus said. He handed her back to her nursemaid. "Goodbye, Mary. I do not know when I will see you again."

"Then I will go now," said Taktu, "and make further arrangements with you tomorrow." He turned abruptly and walked alone toward Minnegarha. The nursemaid also turned and headed back with little Mary.

An internal earthquake jolted the young prince, and a great abyss opened between Vima and his father.

"YOU ARE ALL HERE," CALLED THE SHEPHERD, MAITREYAJNA, who stood by the well. Vima came from his place to be with the others. "It must mean that you all agree to my condition." Maitreyajna tested one of his students, Vima, to see if the boy had the humility to obey him without question.

"I'm very thirsty," Maitreyajna continued. "Vima, fetch me some water."

Vima looked at Jesus and the others, then dipped the community ladle and handed it, dripping, to their new master.

"Thank you, my son," said Maitreyajna.

Looking at the top of the hill between them and Minnegarha, he asked, "Who comes?"

They saw the king's advisor, Wenta, walking hastily with his daughter, Sanum, and another woman. As they drew close, all could see that Wenta was distraught. His left hand held his daughter by the arm. In his right hand he carried a thick bunch of her long brown hair. Finally the trio arrived before Maitreyajna.

"Master," he said, "my daughter will not be reasoned with. She is determined to follow you. Sanum says that she seeks Maitreya with all her life. Last night she cut her hair with her knife and she is now determined to travel with you as a nun."

Her father paused and laid the locks as an offering at the shepherd's feet. "I cannot imagine what her mother will say when I return home without her, but I also know my daughter. She has been trained in the arts of our forefathers, and there is little to keep her with me if she is determined to go. Her life is yours, Master.

"If you accept her, I have requested her matron servant, Lariska, go also. Lariska is close to the royal family and saved the newborn princess herself. She, too, understands your condition, and she is devoted to her young charge."

Wenta paused, waiting for the shepherd's decision.

Maitreyajna looked at Sanum and Lariska. The girl's unevenly shorn hair stuck out in all directions. Her travel robes were plain and peasant-style. Lariska was stout, with ruddy cheeks under graying red hair. Maitreyajna laughed.

"Yes, they may come!" he said. "They, too, will preach."

"Then it is agreed." Wenta embraced his daughter and said goodbye to the others.

Joseph said his parting words to Jesus, who held his great-uncle for a long time. Awa cried outright at leaving his kind master, Joseph.

"Our time is come," said Maitreyajna. "Jesus we will now call Issa, as Awa wisely suggests. Vima is also too famous. We will call you Mitre—a shortened name in honor of the guru Maitreya you seek."

The seven unlikely travelers slowly made their way down the dusty road. Before returning to Minnegarha, Joseph and Wenta watched the cluster of seekers disappear in the distance.

Vima, now Mitre, reeled from his father's abandonment. Everything was new and unfamiliar—his name, his status, and his companions. His only small comfort was that two friends —Sanum and Zhu—accompanied him on this journey he did not want to make.

8

TRAVEL PLANS

A few days later

THE OLD SHEPHERD, MAITREYAJNA, LIMPED AND LEANED
on his staff as the pilgrims walked down the road. Progress
was tedious. The king's son was bored and lagged barely
within hearing distance behind the group. Awa and Lariska
became parental. They admonished Mitre to keep up and
attentively watched the others. Issa and Sanum strolled next
to Maitreyajna. Zhu walked ahead, scouting the road.

Maitreyajna joked lightheartedly. He regaled the travelers
with ancient Hindu, Buddhist, Greek, and Roman stories.
Many times the shepherd stopped to emphasize points. He
told them about Krishna and his beautiful female companion,
Radha. "They were male and female made from the same
flame of God, like two sides of a coin. Krishna led the warrior Arjuna in battle and taught him the path of life and union
with Brahman.

"Issa, tell our friends how King Solomon decided which

woman was the mother of the baby they brought before him," Maitreyajna requested.

"Foolish chatter," Mitre thought. He wondered how Maitreyajna could be the same person who healed him in the cave—or was that a figment of his imagination?

Mitre silently suppressed his unhappiness and thought about the fact that he was hungry. "Where are we going? How many years will it take to get there? How long must we listen to these endless stories?" he asked himself.

Maitreyajna paused and turned to Mitre. "Tales teach people the hidden mysteries of God. We are often blinded to these secrets by the karma of our misdeeds from many lifetimes, which results in self-created suffering.

"Thank God everyone can hear and understand stories. Our minds take in the story while our inner beings—our souls—recognize the truth behind it. In this way, we are enlightened bit by bit."

Issa reflected upon how easy it was to understand Maitreyajna's stories. They were entertaining and applied to everyday life, even though they were based on ancient scriptures and legends. He longed to hear more of them and to weave some himself. As a child, Issa had often noticed how he and his little friends greatly enjoyed the stories told of their forebears. Listening to Maitreyajna moved him, and now he knew that stories would move his friends as well.

The shepherd looked at his followers and continued,

"But you, as sons and daughters of God who seek to overcome your karma, must try to understand the truth directly so that you can awaken others. And the first thing you must know is who you are."

"Awaken others," Issa thought. The phrase caught in his mind and resounded in his heart. "This is a purpose from my Father," he observed.

With his staff, Maitreyajna drew a triangle in the dust of the road, its apex pointing toward his feet. "Imagine this symbol above each of your heads. The descending point shows that the flow of our Father comes from above into your hearts, into the center of your lives, and into the seat of God within you."

Next he drew a second triangle intersecting the first with its base at his feet, forming the six-pointed star. "The ascending point is the nourishment of our Mother that fills the world around us, rising to meet the Father in our hearts. This is the cradle for the flame of the Divine Presence within you—your inner voice.

"The flame is not always easy to hear. Its quiet voice is crowded out when we are hungry, tired, and concerned with cares of the day—or when our monkey-mind is racing from thought to thought."

The monkey, Hanuman, climbed to Awa's shoulder and peered at their leader. Maitreyajna scolded, "Yes, *you*, little friend, teach us about our own minds, always restless and never still."

Mitre sighed impatiently. He brooded over the loss of his family. He was ready to turn around and go back, regardless of the danger. "This we know," he burst out.

"Hold your tongue," Lariska huffed. A few days ago the motherly servant would not have dared speak to the prince in this manner. Today was different. Mitre was dead to the world as royalty. "Not all of us have your training," she said.

Addressing Maitreyajna, she asked, "Do you think I have this flame?" Lariska filled with hope.

"Yes, it is there, giving you life. But it can be snuffed out completely," he warned, "by rage and willful wrongdoing.

"A great teacher shows by his or her actions how a son or daughter of God masters the use of the three flames twined together as one. People observe and learn by example. Students imitate the teacher. When the students achieve mastery, and balance their karma and the flames in their hearts, they no longer need rebirth. They live instead in the real world of God, and they send to struggling humanity waves of illumination they have garnered by their victories over ignorance."

Issa pondered Maitreyajna's lesson. He thought of views his parents and the rabbis shared about the great-grandfather of Noah, named Enoch, who walked with the Father. As a boy, Issa had listened many times to the telling of Enoch's story. The holy man had explained about angels who challenged the Creator and left heaven. These challengers were embodied in the race of men and women.

Enoch's testament said these "fallen" angels enticed the Almighty's children with sensuality and material things. They invented weapons and incited wars, distracting the Father's children further away from Him. The children imitated their actions and must now choose to find their way back. Some would remember their divine heritage. And the fallen angels would be judged one day by Heaven for their acts against these sons and daughters.

Maitreyajna let his students take in his words. "Let's rest," he said. "We will have our refreshment in the shade."

Awa shook his head. There was much to absorb. His tongue went ahead of him. "Refreshment?" he exclaimed. "We are in the middle of nowhere and we have little money for a long trip. Where are we going? And how long will it take?" Mitre could not have put it better himself.

Maitreyajna chuckled. "It is a very long journey to find Maitreya. Don't worry, faithful Awa. We are going first to Mathura to study the sacred Vedas. As for refreshment, it arrives soon," he concluded knowingly.

"But we are looking for Maitreya," Awa objected. "I thought he was the Coming *Buddha,* not a god from the Vedas."

"All true paths lead to the top of the same mountain," Maitreyajna replied. "We can gain elevation from each."

As soon as his sentence ended, Maitreyajna was greeted

by an excited man who appeared where the road crested a hill. He pushed a cart of melons.

"Maitreyajna. You are back," the stranger called. "Welcome. Something told me to come this way. I asked, why am I to go toward Minnegarha with my melons rather than take them to the village market? Now I know. What good news! Please do me the honor of enjoying some of these while I go tell the villagers." He disappeared back over the hill.

Awa stared in amazement after the melon peddler.

ISSA AND ZHU SAT NEAR EACH OTHER ON A LARGE ROOT of the banyan tree. Issa watched as Zhu opened his pouch and took out a small pot the size of a large coin, peeled back the cloth cover, dipped his finger into the salve, and rubbed it into each temple. A fragrant smell of herbs wafted in the hot, humid air.

The smell of the unguent carried Issa to the time of his departure from Nazareth. His mother had carefully bundled herbs for him. She explained their healing attributes—knowledge that was handed down through the generations.

"Why did you choose to come on this journey?" Issa asked Zhu.

A mosquito hummed. Zhu chose his words. "My father was the king's physician and my ancestors healed people. My elders taught me to walk the path of kindness. I must carry on the honor of my people.

"One day Mitre will be king and I will serve him. If I meet Maitreya, he will help me gain wisdom. I believe he lives in the high mountains where I will also learn more secrets of herbs and medicines.

"That is why I came, though sometimes," he confessed, "I long to do more than serve Mitre."

Issa opened the leather pouch he carried and took out one of his mother's bundled herbs. "These are plants from my country. When you're tired, they can be mixed with oil and rubbed onto your feet to soothe them. Soon you feel strong again. I would like to learn the medicines of your people."

Zhu smiled. "You'll have to spend the rest of your life here. There are thousands of cures. I've studied for as long as I can remember. I'll show you some as we go along," he said.

Sanum came with pieces of juicy melon for them. "Aren't you hungry?" she asked.

"And you? Why did you come, Sanum?" Issa asked. They bit into the dripping slices.

Sanum sat down next to them. "When I saw Maitreyajna, I knew him. Right away I wanted to follow him and be a devotee, even though I was trained to be part of the court of King Taktu and his son." She looked at the ground. "Perhaps I can do more as one who renounces the world and prays for others. Maitreya will tell me. And for now, I obey Maitreyajna."

"Ooohpaah!"

Sanum turned to see Mitre charging her from behind with a stick he held for a sword, twirling it over his head.

"Mitre, stop playing," she called. But the boy continued running toward her.

As he charged, Sanum swung slightly to grab one of his arms and, bending still further, pulled hard and Mitre tumbled in the dirt. He landed on his back before Issa and Zhu. Hanuman raced from the other side of the tree. The monkey screeched, clapped, and squatted next to Mitre, who lay snickering.

"I knew you would do that," Mitre boasted. "I just wanted to see if a nun still knew how to fight." He sat up and dusted his shoulders.

Sanum flushed. "Don't be stupid. All day you have dragged along and complained. Now one of us could have been hurt."

Mitre mocked her. "I could have been hurt, poor prince!" He frowned and added irritably, "I am not as interested in journeys as all of you are. I want to go home and have my sister raised as a princess, not as a foreigner. What is wrong with my father?" he nearly shouted. Embarrassed, he wiped his eyes.

Issa put his hand on Mitre's shoulder. Since childhood Issa had possessed an unusual ability to feel the pain of others. When his mother noticed her little boy's anguish over a hurt child or animal, she warned him to guard his feelings.

But the young Jesus always wanted to help, no matter the cost. Once, when he was five years old, he cried all night because he had been impatient with a playmate who then left their game in tears. He agonized over the pain he had inflicted and wondered what he could do to soothe it and make amends. In the morning he ran to apologize. For many weeks afterward he eagerly worked side by side with his friend, taking on the boy's chores and then completing his own.

Compassion had not left him now that he was in his teens. Issa was driven by a desire to ease the burden of others' sufferings.

The prince sobbed. Issa waited.

"Mitre, in the Creator's kingdom, there is no separation."

"What do you mean?" Mitre rubbed his sleeve across his cheeks.

Sanum leaned in to hear Issa.

"We are all connected. We are never alone. Your father is blinded now by his grief, but one day he will see, with your help."

Mitre knew what Issa prophesied was true. He was surprised that his loneliness softened in the presence of this new friend.

Sounds of giggling came toward them from a group of three young women dressed in bright saris. As they walked, silver bracelets and ornaments jingled on their bare arms and ankles. One girl carried a garland of fragrant, white gardenia flowers. Several young children marched behind, shaking small hoops with little bells and tassels tied to them. Following them all was an elephant and her handler.

As the procession approached the banyan tree, the melon peddler brought up the rear, dramatically waving his hands to move the parade along. When all stopped before the banyan, he mopped his forehead with the lower corner of his tunic and said, "As the official greeter of the village of Punjura, I welcome you, esteemed Maitreyajna, and your guests to join us." He pressed his palms together and bowed. Awa ran to Issa to translate into Aramaic.

The elephant knelt and the handler, wearing only a loincloth, eagerly motioned to Maitreyajna and the others to mount.

Issa's eyes widened. He leaned toward Zhu and asked, "What animal is that?"

Mitre overheard and quipped, "You foreigners have a lot to learn. That is the great dragon of the mountain gods. Only the most holy men can tame them. With one twist of that long nose, they can twirl you in the air and toss you away like a twig. No problem for someone like you, who always listens to the flame in his heart," he said, sarcastically. The moment these words left his lips, Mitre regretted them, and was baffled at why he would hurt someone he respected.

Sanum interrupted. "Elephants are used here for work and riding. I think Mitre is the dragon of the mountain gods," she countered with an exasperated glance at her childhood friend.

The girl with the garland of gardenia flowers draped it over Maitreyajna and took him by the arm to the elephant. Maitreyajna climbed up with the help of the keeper. He straddled the beast close to her head. Zhu helped Issa move behind Maitreyajna, and then Mitre boarded, happy at last to be riding something. Besides missing his parents and sister, Mitre also missed his horse.

The others gathered around, and the elephant carefully raised herself. With a commotion of jingling hoops and songs to Krishna, the entire entourage proceeded toward the village.

9

A STRANGE ENCOUNTER

The same day

PANUM SRI BASHIR SIPPED SWEET TEA AS HE LOUNGED
on a stack of plump cushions. He stared sleepily through the
opening of his tent. His bronze hands contrasted with the
immaculate white of his long-sleeved tunic. A thick gold ring
with the head of a cobra chiseled into a black onyx stone
dominated the index finger of his right hand. His black beard
was neatly trimmed under his chin, cutting a fine definition
against his garment.

Bashir's face was oval and smooth, though he approached
midlife. His upper lip was clean shaven, and dark eyes bal-
anced the blackness of his beard.

His circular white tent was pitched with a group of four
others on the outskirts of Punjura. Bashir was making his way
to the coast to buy imported jewels. A landholder, his estates
were inherited through his bloodline of warlords.

Business was simple. He leased land to farmers and

garnered a percentage of crops. Hardened overseers acted as managers of his holdings near Mathura and in other regions. Trade in jewels was another profitable avenue of Bashir's far-reaching enterprises.

This afternoon he rested before resuming his journey.

Bashir snapped his fingers and called, "Lahore!"

A beautiful teenage girl, with head bowed, appeared at the opening. Her face was expressionless. Noting his empty cup, she disappeared and came back with a brass teapot. Lahore glided in with her eyes averted to avoid the gaze of her master.

She was dressed in red silk trousers that tapered at her brown ankles. Jewelry jingled over each sandaled foot. Her red tunic was woven with borders of golden-thread designs at the hem and neck. Lahore's black hair glistened with rose oil and was pulled under a red gossamer veil. Her deep-set eyes were lined with charcoal powder that extended at the outer corners in tiny upward curves.

Bashir watched intently as she entered. "My women have done well with her," he thought. As she bent to pour his tea, Bashir ran his hand along her calf and up to catch her wrist. Lahore recoiled and took a step back, turning toward the entrance, but Bashir held tightly and pulled her toward him. Frightened, Lahore gasped and dropped the teapot.

Bashir laughed and tightened his grip. "Remember who you are. Yesterday you were a dirty flower weaving carpets—

until I spotted you." He pulled her down, wrapping his arm around her waist and burying his face in her neck. He savored the rose scent.

"Be grateful," he whispered. "The gods have smiled upon you and made you rich. You would never have bettered yourself in this lifetime if I had not uncovered your charm." He clasped the back of her head and pushed her face toward his.

Lahore turned sharply away. "Please—I want to go home, sir."

Bashir was far above her in caste. Her life and the lives of her family were at his disposal.

The day before had been very hot. That morning Lahore, her two younger sisters, and her mother had been sitting before a tall loom in the shade of an awning that extended from their one-room mud hut. Behind the hut her father had been stirring a large, steaming vat of silk cocoons that floated and swirled in the hot water.

Together the matron and daughters were working on a large silk rug. Lahore's mother sang out the color of thread and number of passes for each strand of silk to run through the vertical strings.

As she worked, Lahore's mind wandered to arrangements her parents had made for her marriage. The groom's family had visited a week before and admired the fine carpet on the loom. They agreed to a similar one, though smaller, as the dowry for Lahore. Although Lahore did not know the groom, they glimpsed each other during formal conversations of their elders. A sandal maker with tousled hair and protruding teeth, he was a few years older than Lahore. She guessed he was kind. Lahore thought her parents found a good match.

Her musings broke when a group of men on horseback rode in front of the hut and suddenly stopped. Before her was Panum Sri Bashir, a stranger to them all, staring at Lahore.

It was the land baron's pastime to wander the last village of his day's journey and find a lower-caste girl to suit him. Muscular guards carried the prize to camp, where Bashir's servant women cleaned and dressed her. If a girl pleased Bashir, he kept her for a while in his entourage. If she did not, he gave her to his guards.

Bashir, in white, was conspicuous between his guards. A scimitar gleamed in the red sash at his waist. A long whip was coiled in his right hand. When he held up his arm and pointed at Lahore with the butt of the whip, sunlight flashed off the onyx ring. Lahore's hands fell from the loom to her lap and her mouth dropped open.

The men jumped down and rushed under the awning, trampling silk skeins and knocking over the loom as they grabbed Lahore by each arm. Her mother screamed. The two sisters hid behind their mother.

Hearing the commotion, Lahore's father ran from behind the hut with his wooden stirring paddle in hand. He recognized his impotence to fight. Wailing, he dropped his paddle and raised his hands to the gods. He prostrated himself before Bashir and pleaded for his daughter. He offered a carpet every year for the rest of his life.

Bashir smiled darkly as he relished the scene. The pleading delighted him, as did the trembling family in the background. The men hoisted Lahore up in front of one of the riders. Bashir cracked his whip over her father's back and paused long enough to see if blood came. Satisfied with the torn shirt and the scarlet streak, Bashir kicked his horse, and the caravan went on to camp.

NOW BASHIR WANTED HIS PREY. "PLEASE, SIR, LET ME GO home. I can pay you with silk. I beg you." Lahore struggled to free herself.

But this was the height of Bashir's pleasure and power. He swore at Lahore and turned angry. He tightened his grip and pulled the girl closer. Outside, Maitreyajna's travel party had reached the outskirts of the village. Awa noticed that Hanuman was nervous and fidgety. The monkey scrambled onto Awa's shoulder and peered furtively at their surroundings. He seemed suspicious.

"Look at this!" Awa declared to Lariska. "I say that Hanuman *is* a nature spirit, and I don't care who believes me or not. He always knows when something is wrong." He turned to the animal. "What is it, friend?" he cajoled. "If only you could speak human, you would save me a lot of worry."

The monkey riveted its attention on a round white tent. Hanuman's suspicion mounted into determination. With a squawk, the creature leapt from Awa's shoulder and charged for the tent.

"Hanuman!" Awa called sternly after his charge. "Come back here!"

INSIDE THE TENT BASHIR HEARD A WILD SCREECH AND felt something land on his back. Next came a strong bite on his neck and clawing at his eyes. There was a cacophonous din of drums and symbols outside. The land baron's mind crashed back to his surroundings. He shouted in pain and reached with both hands to protect his eyes.

Lahore seized the opportunity and raced from the tent. Bashir's whole staff stood distracted outside. They were watching the procession of the elephant carrying holy men. They wondered about the old man wearing a garland as he rode along. Who could this be who was honored with three young girls walking in procession, shaking hoops with colored ribbons? Their intense curiosity worked to Lahore's advantage. Panting in terror, she moved unnoticed and thanked the gods for saving her. Quickly running to the abandoned women's tent in the camp, Lahore found her simple clothes and hurriedly put them on, leaving the red silk and jewelry in a pile on the floor. She slipped under the back canvas and circled the village, hiding behind the trees, afraid to approach her home. Bashir would surely come there.

Inside his tent, the master whirled free from the attacker. He opened his eyes when he felt something drop from his back. Bashir bolted for the sword. Then he saw the monkey scamper out of his doorway. Bashir cursed and violently kicked the fallen teapot after the animal.

Accustomed to rage, Bashir was adept at using it. He went to a wooden chest, took two sticks of incense, and called one of his servants to light them in the cooking fire. In the distance he saw the elephant and noisy procession, with a monkey running after it, turn into town.

Bashir took the lighted incense and placed it in a holder before sitting on the cushions. He gathered his anger and focused it on the monkey. The incense burned down halfway.

Awa had lagged behind to capture his wandering friend. He was relieved at last to see the monkey running toward him, when suddenly the creature let out a terrible shriek and fell lifeless. "Hanuman!" Awa shouted. He scooped up his friend and pressed him close. "Hanuman. Come back. What has happened to you?" His tears dropped onto the animal's fur.

Bashir felt his first objective complete. He took a deep breath and turned his rage on Lahore.

The girl hid in the trees behind the village. Fear gripped her, and she wondered how many days it would take Bashir to forget her and leave Punjura. Her heart pounded and her throat constricted. Lahore coughed and clutched her throat. Her chest hurt. She fought for air and staggered from the trees into the square, where the parade of elephant and people had stopped.

Seated high on the beast, Maitreyajna saw Awa below with the lifeless Hanuman in his arms. In the square, the shepherd observed the girl fall on her knees.

Maitreyajna closed his eyes and chanted, *"Om Tat Sat Om"*—I AM THAT I AM—in a resonant stream. He perceived hatred confronting the light of his inner temple. The old man's body felt heavy.

As he continued, the light he invoked increased until it was greater than the oncoming darkness. He concentrated on his vision of luminescent white and blue scintillation and directed it around his companions, filling the square and enfolding the girl. Villagers gathered.

"Darkness," Maitreyajna commanded out loud, "by the power of God in me, you are rolled away and returned to your sender."

Lahore breathed normally. She lifted her head and stood up slowly. Bewildered and frightened, she looked up to understand her delivery and recognized Maitreyajna. She dropped to her knees again and bowed until her head touched the earth. "A million blessings from the Goddess Lakshmi to you, great guru. She sent you to save me."

The handler signaled the elephant. She folded her knees, and her passengers disembarked. Maitreyajna took Lahore's hand and said, "Stand, my child. It is good that you thank the Divine Mother. I have done nothing. Only God can reverse the tide of black magic."

Lahore saw Awa cradling Hanuman, the monkey's limp arm dangling. Struck with grief, she went to Awa and placed her hand on the pet's head. "This little one rescued me," she said. Lahore told them of the attack on Bashir.

Still concentrating, Bashir could not understand why his image of the girl became clouded. He was sapped of strength and his head ached. When he reached to put out the incense, his hand trembled. He sank back on the cushions and rubbed his temples. He knew someone had blocked him. The realization made him shudder.

The headache worsened. Bashir fumed. He stood, grabbed his whip, mounted his horse, and turned toward Punjura, motioning three men to ride with him.

The crowd in the town center grew, and people quickly circulated the heroics of Hanuman. They called him holy and placed him on a mat of woven palm leaves. Many brought flowers and piled them on top of the little body until only the face showed.

"God created nature spirits," Maitreyajna taught. "They usually work unseen to tend our physical world, but sometimes they are in animal bodies.

"These childlike spirits are our friends and they sacrifice for us. When they are attacked by dark forces, they are defenseless. Pray for their protection.

"Awa," the shepherd continued, "Hanuman defended this girl. Nature spirits advance by serving life. May Hanuman be blessed for his action." Awa nodded in understanding but his broken heart was inconsolable.

Maitreyajna and his group rested on mats brought by the people. Everyone shared the fruit and bread being passed through the crowd.

Issa felt anxious. He intuited a dark presence and strained to see who approached. Bashir, on horseback, broke into the ring of people. The land baron's dark eyes were scratched across the lids. He scanned the circle until his glare landed on Lahore.

Instinctively Issa moved in front of her. The crowd became silent.

Issa spoke in Aramaic. "We know your interest in this girl. I rebuke you in the name of my Heavenly Father. Now leave this place."

Awa blanched and hesitated to translate, but Bashir knew Aramaic. Bashir sneered as he observed Issa—a boy of fourteen. Lahore shook. Bashir uncoiled the whip and snapped it at his side.

Maitreyajna sat quietly. "Sir," he said, "you err to challenge my student. You thereby challenge God in me. For this you will someday know the wrath of my Father, unless you choose his path."

Bashir blinked, humiliated to meet his match, Maitreyajna, in public.

"Go in peace," said Maitreyajna, "and do not return to the town where you have offended God."

Bashir clenched his teeth. The ache intensified and pounded in his head. He wanted to flail at Maitreyajna, but resisted. Color drained from his face. Bashir abruptly left, followed by his men.

Maitreyajna motioned for Issa to sit with him. "Be patient, my son," he said. "You made a good decision to protect the girl. However, you must know the degree of darkness you deal with before you rebuke one like this. You must become the fullness of the God within. This takes prayer, fasting, study, meditation, and faith."

Issa had been taken aback by his own boldness. "Where did my words come from?" he asked himself. It was the same tendency as in his childhood. Words came and he spoke them, regardless of the possible consequences. The impact of his challenge to a powerful person only now sank into him. He shuddered at the thought of what would have happened had he challenged a Roman centurion. Maitreyajna's gentle chastisement and lesson to him was like salt in a wound. And how could he expect Maitreyajna to come to his rescue whenever he encountered danger? Issa flushed as he reflected on his actions and his master's words.

"Your time to challenge him and others is not come, though it will," Maitreyajna concluded. "Soon we will arrive in Mathura and your studies will begin."

ON HIS WAY BACK TO CAMP, BASHIR STORMED INTO A small temple and confronted several priests. "Do you have a scribe?" he bellowed, seething with anger. One priest acknowledged that he could write.

"I need a message delivered immediately to the head priest in Mathura. Write it for me and take it personally to him."

The scribe brought his instruments and flattened palm leaves. Bashir knelt on a mat. He noticed that he was in front of a statue of Lakshmi. "Cold stone," he thought, "you are helpless. And I have patience."

Bashir vowed he would exact his revenge—no matter how long it would take. He prided himself in never forgetting or leaving a vendetta incomplete.

10

MATHURA CROSSROAD

Mathura, central India, two years later

ISSA SAT CROSS-LEGGED IN THE WALLED GARDEN OF A large Hindu temple. A small wooden writing tablet was on his lap. The grounds were quiet except for doves calling beneath the bushes and the sweep of Awa's twig broom on the stone pathway.

Every day for two years, Issa had studied language and religion with the monks. In the beginning he wondered why Maitreyajna insisted on this rigorous, disciplined tutoring. Day in and day out, reading, discussing, and copying. But now Issa's mind was engaged and challenged as he related his readings to the world around him.

Mitre, however, found the time tedious. The boy harbored resentment and anger toward his father, and he felt hurt by Taktu's actions. These emotions were confusing. Mitre's young mind was not equipped to sort out all of the feelings. Further, he sometimes haughtily complained to his friends that his true calling was to be king of the Kushans, *not* a priest—although no one expected Mitre to spend his life in a temple. He was often asleep or missing from class, and he would have disappeared altogether had it not been for Issa regarding him as a younger brother, explaining the lessons in simple terms, and taking him on forays into Mathura.

Describing facets of Brahma, Vishnu, and Shiva as Father, Son, and Spirit to Awa and Mitre made Issa awaken more and more with his desire to bring truth and illumination to people of every walk of life—including the poor, who had no direct exposure to these ideas.

Today, satisfied with his work copying a Vedic text, Issa stretched his spine, relaxed, and twirled a twig between his thumb and forefinger as he considered how to communicate another profound concept. He leaned against a tree. "Awa," he called, "come see what I have written."

Awa paused behind Issa and peered over his shoulder. "Master, I am not allowed to see these things," he said.

"Awa," Issa said, laughing, "please sit down. Every day I tell you what I have learned. Nothing has happened to you. No one questions my business with you."

"I feel the priests are waiting for the right time to pounce upon me," Awa answered nervously.

Issa remained quiet and looked thoughtfully at his helper.

Awa knew there was nothing that could take him from his master's side. The foreigner treated him as an equal and a student, not as a servant. Issa was calm and caring.

Awa couldn't quite place the otherworldliness that sometimes surrounded his charge. But, at the same time, Issa was still a youth, and Awa had observed in him a stubborn streak and an untempered directness—even flashes of anger at injustice and hypocrisy. The young man often spoke of his family and his cousin John, a best friend. "John and I dream of lifting people out of abjectness," he once said, without elaborating. Awa knew Issa missed his people greatly.

He sensed that Issa was on a search for something intangible—an identity that had not yet completely matured. Would they ever find a guru to help unlock Issa's knowledge from past lives and guide his youthful ardor? Did such a wise young man need a teacher at all?

Issa continued, "Truth is for all. When I see the poor of this land struggling and suffering, I cannot deny them the comfort that the scriptures offer. I am compelled to speak to them. What is the point in studying unless it is to give peace and hope to others?

"Today my Father gave me greater understanding of our oneness with him. Tonight I will teach again in town. Listen. In the beginning was the Word, and the Word was with the Father, and the Word was the Creator. The Vedas say the beginning was Brahman, the father god, with whom was the female, Vak, or the Word. She is in him and of him. She expresses as the Word, the power of the Father—his creation.

"I am the Word, Awa. You are the Word. Every son and daughter of the Most High is the Word—the incarnation of the Almighty in human form. If every person understood this, it would be his or her salvation, the key to understanding that the Father and the Word are in them, too.

"For their sakes, I must demonstrate this to the world, and you must be like me also."

Awa scrunched his face and scratched his head.

"Tonight I will speak of the Om and the power of the Creator that rolls through the universe as we intone the sacred sound to encompass all of life."

Issa's tutoring was interrupted when a priest came from the temple, pulling Mitre alongside him. The boy laughed. The priest tugged Mitre's ear and loudly reprimanded him.

Marching the young man straight to Issa, the instructor fumed, "Here is your cohort. He drew a picture of our head priest." The monk threw a flattened palm leaf at Issa's feet. Issa turned it over. Upon it was a crude sketch of a donkey with a man's head.

"He thinks he can get away with anything because he has a wealthy patron who pays the temple," the man continued. "Well, I don't care about patrons, so do not try my patience. I hold you responsible for his behavior. Go now—all of you. This boy must come back with his lessons perfect, or he will not be admitted again." The livid disciplinarian hurried back into the temple.

Issa gathered his materials and stashed them inside the building. Then, after collecting his two companions, he led them outside the gate and toward town. Issa was silent, brooding. Mitre glanced sideways at his mentor, sensing that Issa's deep thought was about his own unruly behavior. To cover his guilt, Mitre usually chose among a humorous antic, a dramatic display of innocence, or an outrageous statement that swiftly changed the subject. He never premeditated these responses. They came to him reflexively, as a form of relief to whatever was uncomfortable in his life at the moment. His discomfort intensified now, however, because no escape mechanism popped into his mind. During the awkward silence—with even Awa holding his tongue in exasperation—Mitre fished around frantically for something nonsensical to say or do.

"Don't even try," Issa said sternly.

"What?" Mitre asked, feigning astonishment.

"You know what." Issa turned and confronted the boy, stopping their walk. "How long do you expect people to laugh at your jokes when they are meaningless? They have nothing to do with making you or anyone else a better person."

"Do you want to get us all kicked out?" Awa chimed in.

Mitre was used to Issa being patient and tolerant. This was different. Issa's eyes flashed with indignation and his expression was serious as he stood erect with his hands at his sides. That gaze penetrated straight through the mischief-maker. Mitre squirmed.

"The Signet," Issa asked, "does it mean nothing to you?"

"I didn't ask for it," Mitre replied petulantly.

"Go ahead," Issa continued, "throw away your birthright as a son of the Almighty, all because your feelings are hurt. We are not on this sojourn to learn the alphabet, as you seem to believe. I see it by your boredom. We are here to grow in wisdom. We will need it." Abruptly, Issa turned again toward town, striding onward with Awa at his side.

Mitre's feet wouldn't move. He put his hands on his waist and hollered, "What am I supposed to do?"

"You decide," Issa called over his shoulder. "Stay and grow, or leave and lick your wounds."

"You expect me to be perfect!" Mitre retorted.

Issa stopped again and faced Mitre. "Perfection belongs to the Father," he said.

Mitre observed that although Issa's voice was stern, his countenance had softened. The younger boy was comforted.

"*I* do not expect you to be perfect," Issa continued, "but to strive to be more like the Father, who *is* perfect and who loves us in spite of our weaknesses." Then he added, more softly, "Don't you know that I love you as a brother? I need you and I want you to stay. But it's not up to me."

Stunned, Mitre could think of nothing to say.

Issa and Awa resumed on their path.

After a few moments of reflection, Mitre trailed behind, not at all certain as to what decision he should make. But he was certain of one thing: Issa's caring would be a permanent part of him, like a healing salve.

FROM THE LATTICED WINDOW OF HIS SECOND-STORY room, the head priest, Vali, had silently watched the trio leave the garden. He frowned. The shepherd-teacher, Maitreyajna, arranged the boys' entrance at the temple and was the intermediary for an unknown patron.

However, two years ago, shortly after his new students had arrived, Vali had received a memorable and troubling message from his own sponsor. It had been delivered by a scribe from Punjura, and read only:

> *YOUR REALM NEEDS BETTER WATCHING,*
> *BROTHER. A HOLY MAN AND HIS DEVOTEES*
> *MAY DECEIVE YOU. THE GODS WOULD NOT BE*
> *PLEASED AND MAY WITHHOLD THEIR DELI-*
> *CACIES. SEE TO IT.*
> *PANUM SRI BASHIR*

Vali's ample stomach churned.

Discipline problems with Mitre and concerns about the mysterious pilgrim, Issa, were mounting. Bashir's message had returned to his mind. "Did these boys offend Bashir?" he wondered. "How? If they were the subjects of Bashir's threat, what better place to keep an eye on them than under the tutelage of my men?" Besides, the income was good, and

Awa helped with the temple work.

Vali was sure no one knew about his midnight meetings with Bashir, who had made arrangements for the cleric to enjoy women. In return, the influential headmaster opened doors among powerful lords for Bashir's businesses. The prospect of Bashir's wrath shattered Vali's ease, especially since word had arrived that Bashir would return to Mathura in a few days.

Turning from the window, Vali worked his countenance into a benevolent smile. He rang a bell that rested on a carved teakwood table. His aide quickly appeared in the doorway.

Vali was comforted by the sight of his servant. "Murtivra, it is time for our young students to graduate. Inform them that their studies have come to an end, then arrange for them to go on a pilgrimage to the birthplace of Lord Krishna.

"And Murtivra," he added, "follow them tonight and report on their activities to be sure they are pure students of the Vedas. I have heard rumors that Issa teaches the common people."

Murtivra smiled, bowed, and left. Emptiness and fear returned to Vali. He shuddered from the top of his bald head to his sandaled feet.

As they entered the town, Issa, Mitre, and Awa entered another world. The dirty streets of Mathura teemed with people and animals. Pungent smoke and the smell of spices permeated the city.

The three wove their way through a congested neighborhood of ramshackle huts. They followed alleys to a crowded, open-air teashop sheltered by a tattered cloth awning.

Ragged men squatted on dirty mats and sipped tea from cracked clay cups. They talked loudly. Women and children clustered together and spilled into the street.

Everyone looked up at the arrival of Issa and his friends. People greeted them and cleared a place. They set a low rickety table before Issa, Mitre, and Awa, treating them as welcome guests. The crowd quieted.

Children scurried in and gathered around. One boy waved his hand and said to Issa, "Tell us more about Moses."

All were eager to hear the young foreigner speak about meaning and hope for their lives.

Issa smiled warmly at the children and nodded respectfully to the adults. "I saved the best part—how Moses met the Heavenly Father." Issa recounted the tale of Moses' journey up a mountain. His listeners intently followed every word.

No one paid attention to the priest on the outskirts of the group. Murtivra strained to hear the story.

Murtivra liked Issa and respected the young man's diligent study of the Vedas. Early during their stay, it was Murtivra who sat with Issa and Mitre one afternoon under a large spreading tree. Mitre said, "You have so many gods. It is too confusing."

Murtivra had laughed good-naturedly. "The many gods are simply different personifications. Behind them there is one reality, Brahman."

"The Jews worship one Heavenly Father," Issa commented. "Is this your Brahman?"

"Precisely," Murtivra replied. "The One is the One for all, and we are part of him. Our problem is that we humans have forgotten our divine nature. We have become attached to our individual selves and our station in life. In trying to fulfill our desires, we often forget to keep things in balance. Some become greedy for money or power or pleasure. We create karma by wantonly feeding our human passions at the pain and expense of others. Then we are destined to be reborn until we pay back the spiritual and physical debts we have created. This is an unchangeable law."

Issa reflected. "Our ancestors said, 'An eye for an eye. A tooth for a tooth.'"

"Precisely!" Murtivra responded.

Issa frowned. "But why are the Sudras and the poor prevented from learning?" he pushed.

Murtivra looked irritated. "Don't you see? It is their karma from past lives to be born as Sudras—not the fault of priests. They are paying their debts."

"Is there no forgiveness?" Issa challenged.

"It is the law," Murtivra insisted, surprised at his own defensiveness.

Issa looked dejected. He rubbed the light beard growing on his chin. His eyes were sad as he turned to Murtivra. "Is there no hope? They have a divine nature. I think someone should help them with their karma until they can learn to do better."

Mitre watched the debate with interest. He had witnessed Issa's respect for the downtrodden as equals. Now he hoped Issa's compassion would prevail with Murtivra.

Murtivra rocked his head from side to side and clucked disapprovingly. "They made their karma. They are the only ones who can balance it. The law is the same for all of us. Eventually the pain of karma wakes us up."

"We could wake them up sooner," Issa said, "with our words."

"It is forbidden!"

"Then by our actions," Issa continued.

Murtivra enjoyed sparring with the earnest pupil, and he was moved by the goodwill Issa intended.

"Perhaps there is a way," the priest relented. "It may be possible that the people's karma could be held back for a time if someone sacrificed greatly on their behalf."

Mitre watched as Issa wrapped his arms around his knees and furrowed his brow in concentration. "What is he thinking?" the prince wondered. Mitre ventured to suggest an example. "You mean if robbers attacked your friend whose karma it was to be attacked, but you threw yourself in front of your friend and took the knife instead? In this way your friend would be spared the returned karma for a time?"

"Yes," Murtivra conceded. "Something like that, or greater."

MURTIVRA NOW HAD A JOB TO DO HERE IN THE TEASHOP. His report was due. Explaining holy things to the common people, as the young man was doing, was strictly forbidden. Murtivra noticed his palms sweating. "But this is not explaining the sacred Vedas," he thought. "It is only the Hebrew god."

Murtivra left the crowded shop. He was satisfied that he had a good report for Vali.

Sanum and Lariska entered the shop, with Zhu following close behind. All three had shaved heads and wore the saffron robes of Buddhist novices.

Issa smiled at them and continued, "Then, Moses saw a bush that was on fire. 'What is this?' Moses thought. 'I see a fire but the bush is not burned. How can this be?'"

He lifted his palms and leaned forward. The children in the crowd were entranced. Many had wiggled away from their parents and moved to the front of the circle around Issa. They stared at the young speaker and their faces reflected the excitement of his animated story. Mitre and Awa were as captivated as the rest of the audience.

"Suddenly," Issa continued, "the fire in the bush spoke.

It was the voice of the Creator.

"'Moses, Moses! Take off your shoes. You are standing on holy ground.'"

A small girl interrupted excitedly, "We take off our shoes when we visit Krishna's shrine."

"Yes," said Issa as people laughed, "you are right."

Issa told them the Lord commanded Moses to go to Egypt and demand that Pharaoh set the Hebrew people free.

The audience gasped, chattered, and laughed with incredulity. "Command a pharaoh to set the slaves free?" they reasoned out loud. "Unheard of. Slaves are Sudras. They are slaves because of their karma. Why didn't Hebrews accept their lot and pray to be born better in the next life?" They shook their heads.

Issa went on. "Moses asked in amazement, 'Who am I to bring the children of Israel out of Egypt? When they ask the name of the god who sent me, what shall I say?'

"The Maker replied, 'Tell them my name: I AM THAT I AM. I AM sent you.'"

There was a moment of silence while people struggled to understand. Smoke rose listlessly from the stove.

"Truly," Issa finished quietly, "the Father gave his name to all people so they would understand that he lives in each one. You are created equally from his light and fire. When we use the words 'I am,' we say his name. When we speak, we use the fire of the Almighty from our hearts. When we chant Om, we use the word of the Most High to create peace and understanding.

"It is written in your Vedas: 'In the beginning was the Word, Vak, who lived with Brahman and was Brahman.'"

The people murmured. Could they be equal to other castes? How did this foreigner know? Should they believe him?

A small, wiry man had an idea. He called, "Master, if the Hebrews were freed as slaves, shouldn't we also be free to become wealthy and study the Vedas? We should rise up against our overlords. You will be our leader. We will make you our king." The man looked around, expecting others to applaud his plan.

Issa looked at him with kindness. "This man wants me to be a *king*," he thought, perplexed. "I share with him truth that should be free to everyone, and for this he is ready to make me a king. Father, what is the answer?"

"Brother," Issa said, "you have the heart of a warrior. Turn your fervor toward conquering the overlord within. It is the part of us that wants to follow our own desires rather than our Father's will. When you master the internal tyrant, you will know true freedom. In the meantime, we are honored to serve God in others, no matter how lowly our task appears. We do our best to please God and make life better for all with truth and compassion."

Sanum felt her face warm as she understood Issa's words. Two years ago she, Lariska, and Zhu had chosen to enter a

Buddhist monastery in Mathura where they would live, study, and pray. This had been her desire since she had chopped off her hair in determination to become a nun. Her father had laid the silky locks at the feet of Maitreyajna. Then she began the trip with her friends.

The shepherd had explained that each student has a unique path. "The way of the Buddha, the Hebrews, the sacred Vedas—it is good to know them all, and more," he said. "There are many roads to God. If you follow one carefully, you will reach the top of the mountain, but from a different side than the others." Now, she and Lariska were Buddhist nuns. Zhu was a monk.

Sanum recognized that Issa's words echoed Buddha's. "Maybe Issa is a Buddha or an avatar," she thought. She felt a power in his words that she had not felt in any of her instructors at the monastery. She determined to write down his teachings and save them.

Sanum observed Mitre engrossed in the story. Her intuition told her he was healing in the presence of Issa.

A serious girl, no more than twelve, lifted an infant. The girl cried, "Teacher, my mother died giving birth to my baby sister. Why did the gods take our mother? Why did she leave us when we needed her? Is the Creator in her?"

Issa replied, "The Creator is in your mother and your mother is in the Creator." Issa reflected on his Vedic lessons and what his companions had shared about the precepts of

Buddhism. He continued, "Where there is sorrow, there is joy as we balance karma made in this and other lifetimes. This world creates an illusion of separation, but death is not real."

The girl wiped her eyes with the shawl at her shoulders. Mitre thought of his murdered mother and Issa's words.

The crowd was distracted by noises of a horn and drum. A yogi approached. His young assistant walked before him and rhythmically sounded both instruments. When the assistant saw the gathering at the teashop, he stopped, placed a wooden bowl on the ground for coins, and called, "Master Yogi Vrima is before you. Come for blessing."

The bare-chested yogi was slight and sinewy. His long hair and beard were dusty and matted. He walked trancelike into the center of the shop. As the assistant blew the horn, the yogi performed. He contorted his body, standing with bent knee on one foot and pulling the other foot to his neck. He held this posture with his eyes rolled back.

As patrons dropped coins in his bowl, the yogi touched their heads with the palm of his free hand. When donations ended, he unwrapped himself and silently bowed. The unusual pair retreated. The fanfare started again and faded when the assistant turned a corner in search of the next audience.

Issa remained at his table, observing. Even the poorest gave something to the yogi.

Someone called to Issa, "Teacher, can you do miracles? What is your yoga?"

Issa said, "Yoga means a pathway to union with the Maker. There are many yogas.

"Be cautious. Some teachers achieve union with our Creator, and others with darkness. Develop your discernment to know which is which.

"My yoga is to do the will of God and be one with the Father and Mother of Lights. This is my path, which you can also choose.

"Miracles are performed every day by our Father. There is no miracle greater than his presence in your hearts."

Yet another visitor walked into the teashop. It was Maitreyajna. Issa pressed his palms together in greeting. When the shop owner saw Issa and his friends bow to their teacher, he exclaimed, "This is an auspicious day. I will make an offering at the temple." He turned to his wife and added, "And, tomorrow I will charge more for a cup of tea."

Maitreyajna seated himself between Issa and Mitre. "My children," he said, "you have done well. It is time to move on."

There was a collective groan from the customers. The children cried.

"What is this?" Maitreyajna responded to the crowd. "First they will go on a pilgrimage to Krishna's birthplace. All are welcome. Gather on the main road at sunrise." A ripple of excitement and laughter spread.

Maitreyajna spoke to his pupils. "After the pilgrimage we will travel east to the coast and visit Buddha's holy shrines. It will be a long trek."

Mitre looked at Maitreyajna sheepishly. He was glad to be reunited with his unusual guardian. "Bapu, I have studied hard," he said. *Bapu,* he learned, was a term of endearment meaning "little father."

"Good," Maitreyajna replied. "And let this picture of a donkey with a man's head be an end to your artwork," he added, brushing his hand over Mitre's hair.

"When you return from Krishna's birthplace, we will join a caravan to Kalinga. Until then," the old man advised his students, "fast on rice and water. A test of your obedience to me and to your inner direction from the Father awaits you."

Mitre sighed and put his head in his hand. He was accustomed to strange, unpleasant requests from his loveable but unpredictable guru.

THREE DAYS PASSED. THE STUDENTS AND TOWNSPEOPLE returned from their visit honoring Krishna. Two hundred well-wishers thronged Issa, Mitre, Sanum, Zhu, Lariska, Awa, and the others. The entire mass slowly and noisily wound through the slum to the teashop, where Issa hoped to find Maitreyajna.

The owner ran ahead and prepared by clearing space and arranging cushions on a table for Issa to sit above the others. Issa declined the platform until convinced it was the only way the whole group could see him and hear him say goodbye. Reluctantly, he took his place.

The human crush pressed from every direction. People stretched their hands to clasp his. The closest bent their heads against his shoulders. Their tears wet his garments.

Issa was visibly moved by their sorrow. These simple laborers had invested tremendous love and hope in him. Letting them down by leaving wrenched him. Overwhelmed, he touched as many hands as he could, wanting to comfort every individual. Was this the test Maitreyajna said would come?

Adding further to his confusion, people began tossing flowers in the air. Blossoms landed on Issa and his friends and caught in their clothes. The reverence toward Issa equaled the reverence toward a deity. Their warm, sincere praise felt encouraging to the young teacher lonely for his distant friends and family. At the same time, it made him very uncomfortable. Issa winced. A moment came for a decision: encourage the crowd and receive their love or not?

Issa held up his hand. The crowd quieted and pushed back to create a circular space. All waited for him to speak.

Mitre, standing nearby, didn't know what to make of it all. He realized how much he had grown to love Issa, but shoved the thought aside. "I'm starving," he whispered to Awa. Mitre's mouth watered as the owner brought forward a tray of rice, lentils, and flat bread. Others produced fruit offerings for the guests.

Issa turned to Mitre and said, in obedience to the direction of his teacher, "We should not break our fast until Maitreyajna returns." Mitre, already devouring bread dipped in lentils, dropped his hand to his lap and pouted.

Issa didn't know what to say to his anxious admirers, but his mind was clear—he could not encourage their worship of him. Words came spontaneously. "May the blessing of my Father be upon you. Thank you for your generosity and kindness.

"Treat each other as you treat me, and you will always be with me and my Father. Remember, it is not me you love, but the Father in me. It is he who does everything." Emotion swelled among the crowd.

There was a commotion as a pregnant woman hurriedly pushed her way through the people. She pulled a young man and a beautiful girl with her. An older man followed. He carried a brilliantly colored and neatly folded silk rug.

The advancing woman said, "Teacher, I was afraid I would miss you." She fell to her knees before Issa. Issa stood and took her hand. He directed her to the cushions on the table, but she would not rise. "No, master, that seat is not for me. We should make a throne for you and your master. I am Lahore. These are my husband, my sister, and my father. You and your master—and a brave little monkey— saved me in Punjura over two years ago. I beg you to stay in Mathura. How can we live without you? My father offers you my sister, Tamin, in marriage. She is very happy and honored to be your bride. Not knowing your parents, we brought her dowry directly to you—our finest silk rug. Please stay in our beautiful land. We want to listen to your words forever."

The young girl's father nudged her forward. Tamin smiled shyly, her dark eyes glowing above rosy cheeks.

Someone cheered, and then another and another until everyone roared approval.

One person said, "Teacher, your master has not returned. You are free to stay with us."

"Stay," they chanted together again and again.

Issa persuaded Lahore to sit. He was overcome and speechless. Lahore reminded him of his beautiful mother and all the families in Nazareth who had proposed marriage to their daughters. His mother had wanted him to stay. It had been a painful decision, but he had felt called away. He thought how peaceful and happy life would be in Mathura.

Where was Maitreyajna? Issa wanted a few days to think and pray. Didn't his Father want him to have the joy of a family? Lahore's sister was lovely. Mathura was an ancient and holy place to live. Issa ached with longing for everything that was vacant in his life. "Father," he whispered, "what is your will?"

He considered the family, the bride-to-be, and the well-wishers. He was touched. "Yes, I can stay," he reasoned. "I can study and teach. Someday I will bring my new friends and family to Nazareth. My Father will bless this choice."

Still, Issa burned with a contradictory hope he couldn't articulate or understand. He wanted something beyond admirers or a bride. He wanted to accomplish the purpose of his life. "Brothers, sisters," he said in a halting voice, "God bless you." Speaking respectfully to Lahore and her family, he added, "Thank you, but I don't know if your offer is the path my Father intends for me or your family."

Issa was aware of strong emotions building. He inwardly thanked his Father that Maitreyajna was his guru on this journey. He remembered the shepherd was expecting him —commanding him—to begin the next part of his arduous studies. In the midst of his feelings it was difficult to hear whatever subtle message his Heavenly Father might impart to him. Obedience to the human teacher he trusted helped Issa make the right choice, because his heart wanted to stay.

"Excuse my poor and simple words of gratitude and farewell. I must go and prepare for our journey," he said abruptly. It was all he could manage. Swallowing hard, Issa left.

Without conversation, the six travelers made their way to the Buddhist monastery. As they approached, they saw a caravan stopped in the street. Maitreyajna was there, beaming. "You have returned," the smiling shepherd observed, "and victorious after passing the test."

"That was the test?" Mitre wondered.

Maitreyajna put his arm around Issa's shoulders. "We will celebrate with dinner and depart in joyous spirits."

Issa was spent. He sat on a large bundle, consumed by thought. Finally, he drifted into a fitful sleep.

11

GROWTH OF AN EMPIRE

Kapisa, four years later

KING TAKTU LEANED OVER THE BALUSTRADE OF HIS PALACE
and stared across the plain where, years earlier, Huns had
attacked his caravan. He recalled the tragic twist of events
in which he was saved by his young son—only to find his wife
killed by the enemy the same day. Vima still traveled with
Jesus' and Maitreyajna's entourage. Taktu's little daughter
was growing up in a foreign land.

Years of grief, loneliness, and depression had deepened
the lines of Taktu's face. His blue eyes carried determination,
along with a sorrow that did not diminish, even on the rare
occasion of a smile.

This was one of those occasions. Taktu's smile was a
satisfied thin line that turned up slightly as he inhaled the
autumn air. The wind blew strands of graying hair across
his face. He turned to his guest.

"Two things are building the Kushan empire," he said.

"One you see before you—the basis of our cavalry that has expanded tenfold since we met." Taktu waved his arm toward the plain where hundreds of large horses roamed, some shaking their heads and running across the expanse, excited by the cold turn of the weather. "Appakke Nakte has been good to my people."

Joseph of Arimathea stepped closer to the balustrade. "Yes," he agreed. "Even the Roman Empire does not produce such magnificent steeds."

Taktu nodded. "But more powerful than horses or war is this." He let several shiny copper coins drop from his closed fist into the open palm of his other hand. The coins jingled.

"Like the Romans in their domain," Taktu said, "we created currency that circulates throughout the region. Prior to my rule, there were scattered warlords in separate fiefdoms bartering for goods. We stamped Kushan currency and poured it into the cities. People began buying, selling, and paying wages. The stability of our new monetary system tied the empire together and created wealth and allies. My reach grew with barely a drop of bloodshed."

Joseph took one of the coins and examined it. Taktu's profile was on one side, the image of the mounted king on the other. Although in his land the Jews banned images of people or animals from their coins and Herod's money could not carry the face of the ruler, Joseph recognized the importance of Taktu's system. "It was a wise srategy to develop the economy," Joseph said. "I observed the growth of your influence as I traveled in your territories doing business with your currency."

"Come, let's eat," the king said as he guided his guest back into the greatly expanded palace.

THE TWO MEN SAT AT A LOW TABLE NEAR THE FIRE. The king's advisor, Wenta, joined them. "Tell us," Wenta began, "about the little princess."

Joseph glanced at Taktu, wondering if the king would object to discussing his daughter, long ago carried to her mother's homeland. There was much to tell but little that would not break the hearts of his companions.

Already four, Mary of Magdala showed characteristics of a beautiful soul who seemed to possess wisdom beyond her years. Her aunt and uncle had recounted a story to Joseph. "One day when she was three, she overheard some guests discussing the Messiah. It was in the evening. Mary ran out of the house crying, 'Where is the star, Auntie? Where is the star?'

"'What star?' her uncle replied.

"'The Messiah's star,' she insisted.

"We had never spoken to her about a star signifying the Messiah, but she was adamant with us. She stamped her tiny foot and tears welled up in her eyes as she shook her curls.

"'I know him, Auntie. I want to see the star. Uncle, show me the star, won't you please?'

"'You do not know the Messiah,' her uncle said as he hugged her and smoothed away her tears. 'None of us know who the Messiah is.'

"'I *know* him,' Mary retorted, burying her head in her uncle's shoulder and sprouting fresh tears. 'I know him from before.'

"Her uncle and I looked at one another in bewilderment.

"'Perhaps you know him from another lifetime,' I said to console her. 'I believe you will recognize him when you see him again in this lifetime or another.'

"The toddler eased in her uncle's arms and looked forlorn. Her next words astounded both of us.

"'He is my twin.'

"'Your twin?'

"Mary nodded. 'The Father told me we are from his home in heaven and we are twins.'"

Joseph had listened in amazement to the parents' story, scarcely breathing. Now it was his turn to tell them the story of the bright star, the prophecies about Jesus and John, and the purpose of Jesus' studies far to the east.

"'You have told us that Jesus named Mary,' the girl's aunt remarked, 'but how could she remember what the Heavenly Father told her? She is only four.'"

"'These little ones are fresh from heaven,' Joseph replied.

'They retain a lot. Let us pray and be patient to see what God answers.'"

Joseph learned from Mary's stepparents that the child's life was not usually so auspicious or cheery. Since infancy she seemed to carry a wound. She cried often. Mary was usually in trouble, intentionally breaking a vessel, spilling oil, or picking a fight with a playmate. He feared the girl would only become more rebellious. But he kept these thoughts to himself.

To Wenta and Taktu Joseph replied, "We found the queen's sister and her husband in Magdala. They mourned Sarah's death, but did not hesitate to add her baby, Mary, to their family. The town of Magdala has been her world. I met Mary again several months ago. She now has long, curly red hair and shining blue eyes. The princess is a beautiful girl with the look of a warrior."

The group was silent.

"And your son?" Joseph asked Taktu.

Frowning, Taktu reached for a vessel and filled their cups as he spoke.

"I have not seen Vima since I sent him with the shepherd. Our staged murder was successful. No one speaks or thinks of him any longer. To the world he is dead, but everything I do is for him. Someday he will reign over a vast empire.

"Maitreyajna visited me after several years and brought news of the prince's studies of the Vedas and Buddhism.

The hand of Appakke Nakte is upon him. He will be a great king with many people and religions under his rule." Taktu paused and cleared his throat. "If he can forgive my harsh actions."

Joseph gazed into the flame of a lamp on the table. "A paradoxical meeting," he thought. Here they were, all reunited as friends who had suffered losses and sacrifices. He remembered Jesus' mother, Mary, in tears at the recent death of her husband.

A widow now, Mary's life would have been harsh had it not been for her son James and for the care of Uncle Joseph. She had confided to her uncle and to her cousin Elisabeth how she longed for Jesus' return. She clung to her inspired direction to hold the vision immaculate for Jesus. "It is the Father's will for my son to gather as much understanding of the world as possible," she told herself.

She filled her long days with the care of her family and with ministering to friends who were sick or troubled. All considered this extraordinary woman to be strong and stoic, emanating holiness that brought comfort to others even though her own life was one of anxiety and pain.

Joseph had asked Maitreyajna to take word of his father's death to Jesus, but the great-uncle had no idea when or how Jesus would receive the unhappy news.

Feeling unsettled, Joseph opened the leather pouch hanging from his shoulder. He took out several flat palm leaves that had been pressed and used for writing material. They were wrapped in yellow cloth. "Maitreyajna brought a letter from Jesus to his family and friends," he said before he read.

> Peace. I long to see you, Mother and Father.
>
> Pray for me while I am far from the people and land I love.
>
> I still search for my teacher, Maitreya. The shepherd, Maitreyajna, helps me prepare for the Great One. I'm studying the Vedas and Buddhism.
>
> We stopped in Sarnath, a place of pilgrimage for Buddhists, where Gautama Buddha delivered his first sermon. Someday I will share his words in a way that our own people will understand. Great memorial pillars and stupas stand in his honor throughout the land. I have never seen anything like them.
>
> We reached Bodh Gaya, in the northeast, where Buddha became enlightened. I could feel the power of his accomplishment.
>
> I studied Buddha's life in the city where he lived, Rajagriha, and visited the holy cave where he meditated. It is said that Buddha tamed a wild elephant. I have seen these creatures for myself. Buddha developed inner peace that influenced others. He renounced all in himself that was not real but was created by desire.
>
> As I write, we are traveling by boat from Tamralipti in the east. We left the Ganges River delta and

now sail along the seacoast south to Kalinga, where we will visit another holy place.

I hope you can feel my love with you. I will be back.

Greet all who serve my Father. Grace be with you.

Seeing the handwritten proof of Jesus' whereabouts always gave the older man a sense of security. Joseph carefully folded the cloth once more around the palm leaves. "The Father has a unique plan for each of our young ones," he said. "I must be ready to help Jesus fulfill his purpose.

"The Roman rulers are erratic. Their lives and their cities, including Rome and Jerusalem, are degenerate. The people are clamoring for the fulfillment of prophecy. They want a leader. Some want a militant messiah who will overthrow the Romans and take over Jerusalem. Others say the prophets foretold a *spiritual* leader to give them solace.

"Jesus' relative John has gone into the desert and is living as an ascetic. I'm worried about him. He's a fiery one and rails against the vices of our local rulers. John is certain Jesus will return to break the bonds of their tyranny. I believe Jesus' mission is beyond politics, but who knows what the Father has in mind? My role is to be Jesus' guide and protector. For this I need stronger influence with the Romans.

"And you, Taktu, need greater strength to expand your domain for your son's rule of people who will embrace many cultures. This is why I have come with a proposal."

Taktu looked quizzically at Joseph. "Let us have it then," he said.

"I trade in many things," Joseph continued, "but my most profitable and important commodity is metal—tin and precious ore. The business has taken me many places. I am returning now from a new interest in an area of your empire north of Kabul."

Joseph unwrapped a small, white silk cloth and laid a gleaming gold coin in King Taktu's palm. It was roughly the size of the copper Kushan currency.

"Gold," Joseph said, "will tremendously expand the wealth you have established with copper coins and will raise your power, and mine, to a higher level. For you, the riches will solidify your empire and expand the abundance of your people. For me, the venture will give me influence with the Roman emissary in my land."

Taktu held the coin to the lamplight. Joseph continued, "This is a rough sample made from the first ore. It will be years before there is enough to circulate. Men will be needed for this work, along with soldiers to protect them all."

"Done, my friend," said the king. "This cloth we are weaving together will make a fine inaugural cape for my son, or a holy robe for the Messiah your people anticipate."

12

CONFRONTATION AND REDEMPTION

Kalinga, India

As Taktu and Joseph planned their strategies for building protection and a dynasty, across the continent Issa taught. He gave his lessons from the balcony of a home owned by a local family, whose patriarch was impressed by the young teacher. Word quickly spread in Kalinga that Issa was a holy man. Every day crowds gathered from afternoon until evening to hear him. The sensitive student had become an increasingly compelling teacher.

The gradual transformation occurred as the small band traveled through India. During his two years at the temple with Murtivra, Issa gained a brilliant and evident understanding of the holy Hindu texts. Since Sanum, Lariska, and Zhu grew up with Buddhism around them, they had naturally gravitated to those monasteries and donned their robes while Mitre was assigned to remain with Issa. Awa absorbed the words of his friends with a practicality that came from life, which is a teacher in its own right. The invisible grip of Awa's Sudra caste never loosened enough to allow him more formal education with the others.

Then, for two more years, the group was on the move at the behest of Maitreyajna, who mysteriously came and went as he willed. If Awa or Mitre questioned the old man as to his whereabouts, he immediately reminded them of their promises to follow and obey him. "It is your test," he chided, "not to have common curiosity about me. Your hungry mind wants to be satisfied. If you can learn instead to trust me, you can discipline the mind and hear your own inner guru—your true teacher." The subject was dropped.

Maitreyajna directed the travelers to view the holy sites of Buddha's life. He instructed Issa and Mitre to now take up the lessons of Buddhism, and he admonished Sanum, Zhu, and Lariska to guide them to the monasteries along the way and to assist them in their work.

The six covered many long miles, retracing the footsteps of Gautama. As they walked, Sanum filled in details of Siddhartha Gautama's story.

"He was born into the warrior caste near the town of Kapilavastu, in the northeastern part of this land. It was foretold the infant could become a renowned monk, but his royal father wanted Siddhartha to be a great ruler," Sanum explained.

Mitre's ears perked up as the story began to sound a little like his own.

"So," she continued, "Siddhartha's father did not allow his son to leave the palace grounds. He reasoned the boy would never see pain, suffering, old age, disease, or death."

"Well, that ends any similarity to *my* life," Mitre scoffed out loud. "My father *threw me* out of the palace to experience it all." He gestured broadly.

"Your father knows the story of Siddhartha," Zhu noted. "Maybe he didn't want to repeat the mistakes of others."

Mitre had naturally matured, but still he smarted over the sudden abandonment by his father. He clung to Issa's words of comfort and friendship, cherishing them as their relationship deepened. Oddly, the slow healing was creating another change in the young prince. He found himself pondering a new question: When *would* be the right time to return to his father? How would he know? And how could he leave Issa and his friends?

Sanum went on. "But when Siddhartha was grown, he did leave the palace, and he saw all of these sad parts of life. It troubled him greatly and he left everything he loved—his wife, child, and wealth—in order to learn the cause of suffering and how to overcome it."

Now it was Issa's turn to reflect upon *his* life. Like Siddhartha he left family and friends to seek understanding that would help him fulfill his destiny. He observed his sandaled feet as they trod the rough road. They were covered with dirt. His formerly white robe was gray—especially at the bottom—from dust. He felt tired and adrift. When would his sojourn end and his life's work begin?

Currently Issa's life was not one of ease. He and his companions often slept in fields. When money ran out, they carried begging bowls to ask for rice. Mitre was handy with a sling and provided an occasional bird or rabbit for a meal. Issa took carpentry work as he found it and taught Mitre some of the skills of his father's trade. Zhu helped towns-people with his medical skills. The group pieced together their subsistence. Sometimes Maitreyajna replenished their treasury with small amounts of money from Joseph of Arimathea or Taktu. Monks and nuns also welcomed them to their doors.

News of his father's death dealt a heavy blow to Issa. He grieved over not being home for Joseph's last days and to care for his mother. And, there were the nightmares. They had lessened in frequency, but at least once a month Issa awakened from fights with some form of evil or temptation. On other nights he was tormented by the pitiful eyes of diseased adults and starving children. The residue of a fitful night was the mocking voice in his head that said, "Give up. Why do you persist in the hopeless task of helping others? Go home. It's your fault that your father died. Fulfill your duty of caring for your mother." The projections of criticism were more painful than the nightmares.

Nevertheless, as the group wandered and met many

common families, Issa became more and more determined to unlock hope within ordinary people. He shared freely all he had learned and all he knew they could understand of his Heavenly Father. More than words, he gave comfort through a look, a touch, or simply his calming presence. Always his acquaintances felt uplifted, and they began to consider him a holy teacher.

Issa thought of the suffering in his country. His people struggled under the heavy weight of taxation. The authorities crucified those who opposed them. If Siddhartha knew a way to escape, Issa surely wanted to bring it to his people. His determination was reignited.

"I understand Siddhartha's feeling," Issa commented. "There must be a way to help people overcome their suffering." His longing to serve his Father through serving his brethren might be answered. "How did Siddhartha do it?"

Sanum said, "First he tried practicing extreme asceticism. He thought this was the way to enlightenment. But after six years, he had become so weak he almost drowned when he went to bathe in the river. He realized extreme asceticism did not result in enlightenment or the relief of suffering.

"Siddhartha then ate and walked to the city of Bodh Gaya. He sat under a fig tree and vowed not to leave until he had reached enlightenment. He entered a state of deep meditation.

"Some say he continued this meditation for forty-nine days. During this time he was severely tested by the evil Mara, who wanted to lure him with temptations of the flesh or disrupt him with fear. Siddhartha prevailed, however, and at last he attained union with the one Reality. He became 'the awakened one'—the Buddha."

"How did he help others? " Issa inquired.

"He taught," Sanum replied, "like you do. Perhaps that is why you look for Maitreya. He is the Buddha to come. Maybe he is coming within you and will come in many."

Not everyone was happy, however, with Issa's progress. It rankled Panum Sri Bashir that he had been embarrassed years ago by this young, impertinent, and disrespectful scoundrel who had grown and gathered a considerable following. Bashir obsessed over the humiliating experience and reasoned that the core of the Vedas and the lives of the priests were at stake. To him Issa was a defiler and a threat. It was time to gather payback for the liaisons he had arranged on behalf of the Mathura temple headmaster, Vali. Bashir waited to spring his trap and have revenge.

THE FIRST ARRIVALS IN KALINGA WHO CAME TO HEAR ISSA were frequently the poorest, oldest, or sickest. At night workers came from the boats, docks, fields, and shops. Everyone wanted to hear the simple messages of the plain-robed foreigner, whose brown hair fell to his shoulders and soft beard framed his face.

Issa contemplated teachings given to him by a Buddhist master. "There are four noble truths," the monk had said. "Life is full of suffering. Suffering is caused by our desiring things that are impermanent. We end suffering by eliminating desire. And, we eliminate desire by following a path of eight points: right understanding, right thought, right speech, right action, right livelihood, right effort, right awareness, and right meditation."

When Issa, in turn, spoke to his listeners, he put the lessons into his own ordinary terms. "If you want to end suffering in your life, place your attention on the Heavenly Father. While everything else comes and goes, he will never fail you. Treat your brothers and sisters as you would like to be treated. In this way you will not make negative karma, and you will overcome the cycles of rebirth to dwell with the Father. Seek neither poverty nor attachment to excessive wealth. By walking the middle way, you will grow closer to the Father."

As Issa taught, standing on the balcony so all could see, Mitre stood next to him wearing a similar robe. Mitre was almost as tall as Issa, but the prince's thick hair curled around his head and his face showed just a faint beard.

Maitreyajna had recently joined the group and rested inside the house.

Below in the crowd, Sanum and Lariska carried pails of water to the hot, thirsty listeners. The two women, with their shaved heads and the burgundy clothes of their Buddhist order, stood out from the crowd. Awa scurried through the audience and settled disputes as to who was sitting where. He went from group to group, keeping them in order. Zhu, also wearing his Buddhist garb, sat in the back, working his prayer beads and tending to the sick who came to him.

"Master," called a man below the balcony, "let's collect money and build a temple where you can teach."

"It's not me, but my Father who is Master," Issa replied. "And he provides for every need. Give your gifts to the poor and care for one another. You will serve the Father and me."

A woman spoke up. "If all are made of the Creator's light, why are we servants and what can I do to improve the lives of my children?"

"The light of the Almighty is within you," Issa said. "Look for it. As your first priority, seek him and his will. Then all the things that are truly needed by your children will be given to you."

Suddenly there was a shattering interruption.

"This man speaks blasphemy!" someone shouted from the rear of the audience.

Everyone turned at the thunderous cry. There stood the corpulent head priest, Vali, of the Hindu temple where Issa had studied in Mathura. Vali looked nervous and red-faced. On each side of him was an entourage of priests.

But the cry of "blasphemy" did not come from Vali.

It came from the striking figure mounted on a black horse directly behind him. There sat Panum Sri Bashir, who stared at Issa. "Make way for the true priests," Bashir commanded.

The alarmed people jostled apart. The priests, followed by Bashir, paraded to the front of the gathering. The warlord positioned himself under the balcony.

When it was quiet, Vali raised his reedy voice and said quickly, "I condemn this teaching as unlawful. Now go away, all of you." The priest was sweating and looked faint.

"Louder!" Bashir ordered.

Vali gained strength out of his fear. He pulled himself straight and took a deep breath. "I hereby condemn this teaching. Those who listen to these blasphemers will suffer the consequences of the law."

Bashir's guards circled the audience. Some of his men were mounted, others on foot. "Do you hear?" the warlord shouted. "Take them," he yelled to his men.

The guards knew what to do. They tightened the perimeter of the crowd, barring anyone from leaving. Men on foot captured Zhu, Sanum, Lariska, and Awa, pushing and dragging them to the front where the priests stood in a row. Other men surrounded the house to assure there was no escape for Issa and Mitre.

The congregation was frantic.

Hearing the commotion, the old shepherd, Maitreyajna, joined Issa and Mitre on the balcony. Instinctively, Issa placed himself protectively in front of the old man.

Amidst the panic, Bashir called, "Silence!" He cracked his whip in the air. The crowd hushed and stared. Bashir looked disdainfully at Issa and Mitre. "Fools," he said, "you have gone too far with your idiocy, and now you will have the judgment."

Issa spoke calmly. "My Father judges me," he said. "And his judgment is also upon the hollow persecutors of his children."

Bashir sneered, "We shall see. You are a foreigner who offended me many years ago. Now you offend these priests and the gods. You preach holy words to the untouchables. This is a crime punishable by death. But I am merciful. What do you have to say to these charges?"

"There are no barriers to truth," Issa said. "Those who recognize truth will believe what I say. But those who listen to dark voices have plugged ears and cannot understand."

Bashir seethed beneath the veneer of his patronizing smile. "That is just the point," he said, anger writhing through his voice. "And, this one should know better than to try to understand your words." He pointed the butt of his whip at Awa. "A Sudra knows he is never to hear the holy words. Bring him forward." Two guards shoved Awa to his knees in the dirt before Bashir's horse. "Isn't that right, you filth?"

Awa tried to stand, but the guards kicked him back to the ground.

"Bring forward the tools," Bashir said to his men. Turning to the crowd, he bellowed, "Let this refuse be the example to all of you."

The head priest, Vali, felt sick as he considered his own fate at the hands of Bashir if he did not carry out the warlord's plans. "I must sit," he whispered to a priest at his side. Someone seized a mat from another man and pulled it under the shade of the balcony. Two priests lowered Vali onto it. He sat with a thud, panting. The priests fanned his face with the folds of their robes.

A blacksmith arrived with a cart carrying the clay oven of his trade. Fire glowed at the top. The warlord dismounted and called one of his men to take his horse. Bashir sucked in the power he felt from the intensifying fear of the crowd. "Pull the Sudra to his feet," he commanded. Bashir reached for the heavy ladle lying over the top of the fire. He grabbed it by the wooden handle and let several drops of molten lead drip into the flame.

"In our land, the hearing of the holy word by the worst filth is punished by plugging the ears forever. This is your sentence, you who are twice cursed, for I see you have already been punished for your other transgressions," he said, nodding toward Awa's withered hand.

"And you," Bashir surveyed the crowd, "you believe one who is so useless? Have you no better way to spend your days?" He angrily dropped the ladle back over the flame, causing drops of molten lead to fly in various directions.

Bashir gripped another set of wooden handles protruding from the fire. The handles were attached to long iron tongs, which he pulled from the oven. The tongs glowed. He waved the instrument slowly before Awa's face.

"But you have sinned three times. The tongue that spreads blasphemy must be thrown into the fire. We will burn it out of you for good."

Awa felt his knees weaken. This was the moment the small man had known would come. He refused to look at Bashir and instead turned his head toward the balcony.

Awa saw nothing but Issa's face. The Sudra was strengthened. As a guard jerked Awa's attention back to Bashir, Awa closed his eyes to retain the picture of Issa's gaze.

Bashir's voice rang like a shock through the servant's body. "But I am a merciful man. You can redeem yourself. Your sentence can be softened if you use your tongue to make amends. You are given the opportunity right now to tell these people that your Issa is a charlatan and they should run from his words and go back to their lives. Drop his arms," Bashir ordered.

Awa stood on his own with the terrified crowd seated around him. He looked painfully at them and bowed several times.

"Speak!" shouted Bashir, cracking his whip in the dust.

Awa stood taller. "Issa," the little man said slowly, "is a

holy man—a son of the Most High. You and I, who come to listen, are also the Father's children. I gladly offer my tongue and my ears, which come from the Father and which I give as small gifts in return to him and his children."

Bashir was furious. "You will burn in hell," he hissed between his teeth. "Blacksmith—to work. Those who take their eyes off of this punishment will be killed by my men."

The blacksmith came forward and used a small bellows to intensify the fire.

Quietly Mitre climbed to the rail of the balcony. He used the ancient words to alert his comrades below. The cry, "Appakke Nakte!" came from deep within Mitre's being as he jumped from the balcony onto Bashir.

The startled blacksmith fell back. Awa broke free, took the hot tongs, and ran toward the man holding Lariska. Sanum dug her elbows into the stomach of her captor and grabbed the man's sword. At the same time, Zhu bent down and rolled his guard to the ground. Mitre struggled with Bashir. Horsemen rode into the chaos.

On the balcony, Maitreyajna touched Issa's arm. "Follow me without question and learn from me. Another time will come when you must move unseen with your followers. Now, keep your attention upon your Father," he said.

They hurried down the stairs and directly into the fray. No one noticed them. "My students, come," Maitreyajna called. "The people here will be protected."

Mitre let go of Bashir and disappeared into the crowd. The group with Maitreyajna easily walked through the confusion and past the guards.

THAT NIGHT THE SEVEN TRAVELERS SAT IN A CLEARING surrounded by dense trees. A fire blazed before them. Issa lifted the white shawl from his head and placed it on Awa's head, letting it hang over Awa's shoulders. "You are a friend of the Creator's, willing to lay down your life for truth," Issa said.

Awa took the shawl from his head and kissed it, then folded it carefully. "There is no life without truth," he said simply.

The young nun, Sanum, addressed Maitreyajna. "Father, I took a sword today, ready for war. I was wrong," she said regretfully. Zhu silently waited for Maitreyajna's reply. He had also been ready for deadly combat.

"Today you were called to action," Maitreyajna replied. "Another day you will be called to stillness. Know when God calls you to one path or another, and do not fear."

Mitre looked at Sanum. She was beautiful with serenity that had grown over the years. "I couldn't have moved today if you and Zhu had not followed the command of Appakke Nakte," he said. "Zhu, Awa, Issa, Lariska, Maitreyajna— each one of us played our role. You did well, Sister." Mitre respectfully used her monastic title. "You listened to your inner promptings. That's what you taught me when we were children, wasn't it?"

Bushes rustled and the group was startled by the sound of footsteps. A woman, man, and small boy emerged from the shadows. The woman gasped in surprise when she saw Maitreyajna and the others. "Lakshmi be praised!" she exclaimed. Her shock quickly evaporated and she said, "I am Lahore. You saved me from Bashir before I was married, and we met again in Mathura. I prayed for Lakshmi and the God of Issa to guide me tonight."

"What is it, my child?" Maitreyajna asked.

"In Mathura," Lahore continued, "I heard that you traveled along the Ganges River to Kalinga. I convinced my husband that we must follow you. We were in the crowd listening to Issa." Lahore faced Issa. "Today I betrayed you," she blurted. Tears quickly followed.

Lariska moved next to Lahore to comfort her. "What happened?" Lariska asked.

"We were overwhelmed with the words of Issa and this brave man." Lahore bowed her head to Awa. "When the fighting started, many people fled. But my family and I did not move quickly enough. The greatest disaster happened. Panum Sri Bashir recognized me! How can it be after so many years? It makes me sick to think of him. But, even worse, he saw my son, Benja. He grabbed him and drew his sword to his throat. His men seized my husband. 'I should have known that you would follow this Issa,' Bashir said to me."

Lahore lowered her head. "And I said," she continued, "'I don't follow him. I only came to see why a crowd gathered.'

"'You are a disgusting woman,' Bashir said. 'You are defiled in the eyes of Brahman. It is better for you and your family to be cast into hell.' He was ready to kill us. Then he thought again. 'No, I have a better idea,' he said. 'You may live—a living hell, left to beg while your husband and son go to hell before you.' Our brave son never cried as that evil man pulled his sword tighter to Benja's throat. My husband didn't grovel for mercy. But I," she stammered, "I did grovel. I turned and said to anyone who was left, 'Hear me. This Issa is a blasphemer. Go now. Go to your homes and never come again.'

"The people near me eyed Bashir and moved away. He did not stop them. I stood still and said, 'I will do anything you ask.' Under my breath, I prayed to the God of Issa and Moses.

"'What of yours could possibly interest me?' he said, like a fiend. 'You are old and used.' He spat on my face." Lahore turned red as she relived the humiliating scene.

"He loosened his grip on my son and pushed him to me. Then he shouted to my husband, 'Take her and beat her. Leave my sight before I turn my head back, or you will die.'

"Of course we ran. We found you. I beg your forgiveness."

"Our Father tests us with many fears," Issa replied. "And he cares for us with many miracles. He forgives us instantly. Be at peace. The truth grows in your heart and makes you stronger every day."

Lahore's husband, Patrim, pressed the palms of his hands together in respect. He took a pair of leather sandals from his satchel and handed them to his son. Little Benja bowed low and placed the sandals at Issa's feet. Patrim said, "I made them for you while we listened."

Benja picked them up again and held them over his head for Issa to examine. "My father makes good sandals!" the little one exclaimed. At last Lahore smiled and wiped her eyes.

Issa laughed. "They are very fine, and I accept them with gratitude."

"Stay with us," Maitreyajna suggested to the family.

"Thank you, teacher," Lahore replied. "We will sleep here tonight before we start back to our village."

"In the morning," Maitreyajna continued, "the rest of us will begin our journey north to the mountains for final lessons. Remember, now you are learning from me, but I will not always step into your lives. Only your personal mastery and closeness to the Father will save you in times of need. And, even he will not always intercede. Prepare for the choices ahead."

When Mitre heard they would journey to the Himalayas, he once again contemplated making the long journey home instead, but he told no one of his plan.

13

THE GREATEST LOSS— THE HIGHEST GAIN

Kapisa, months later

SEVERAL MONTHS AFTER MAITREYAJNA FIRST ANNOUNCED travel plans to the Himalayas, Mitre at last reached the high city walls enclosing his father's palace. He was accompanied by the motherly Lariska. "It has been a long time since I've been home," Mitre thought.

He relived the pangs of boyhood: his mother's death, his father's hardness, and his infant sister's removal to a foreign land. He thought of Sanum, now a beautiful young woman who had taken Buddhist vows, and the other traveling companions whom he had left behind. "Appakke Nakte," Mitre whispered out loud, "will I ever see any of them again?"

He felt anxious, but he knew this was where he was meant to be. The dusty roads had brought him peace.

Aging Lariska also longed to be home. She decided that steep mountain canyons and high plateaus were no place for her. Sanum was grown and no longer needed an elder companion. Nevertheless, Lariska's decision to leave had been wrenching for Sanum.

Mitre's mind wandered to an earlier time, to the days before his departure from Issa and the others. As they continued to travel through India, Maitreyajna had guided them to ancient shrines and monasteries, where they studied, prayed, and taught. The high, snow-covered Himalayan peaks loomed throughout the group's journey, until finally Maitreyajna said it was time to forge ahead into the mountains in order to reach their retreat before winter.

Mitre knew the next part of the journey was not for him. The hardships of daily living in foreign lands had worn down the keen edge of his anger. The precepts of the Vedas and the Buddhist teachings had soaked into his soul. Mitre's boyish rebelliousness had melted into the realization that he, too, carried a divine spark that could be nurtured by focusing on what was real and permanent. Issa and the others were often living examples of the Father's care, even though they each had to conquer fears, desires, temptations, and the condemnation of others. Friendship taught Mitre forgiveness. Gradually, he understood that mountainside meditations were not for him. He belonged with his father, regardless of past bitterness.

One morning Maitreyajna and Mitre sat alone by a river. Maitreyajna told the young prince that he would be a great king, uniting people from diverse religions with his understanding of their many pathways to the one God.

"No," objected Mitre, "Issa is the true king."

Maitreyajna laughed. "You are wise, Mitre." The unchanging shepherd held up two boney fingers. "There are two crowns," he said. "I believe Issa *will* pass the great tests ahead and wear his Father's crown forever.

"I believe in you, too, my son. You will overcome life's trials if you remember all that you have learned. More important, you must continue to *live* it. I have done what I can to help you. I have scolded you, laughed at your flaws, and encouraged you so that you see in yourself what is of real value and what is not."

The unexpected tenderness overwhelmed Mitre.

That night, in a foothill town, they all drank tea. It was then Mitre softly announced that he would not continue with his friends.

The group went quiet with shock and sadness. Travel without Mitre was unthinkable. He often made them laugh and forget their hardships. They grew up together.

"But you have not met Maitreya," Sanum protested. "He is the goal of our journey. How can you go back now?"

Mitre looked at each of them and said, "I met Maitreya in each of you."

"So be it," Maitreyajna said, nodding assurance to Mitre. "You are attuned to God's timing. There is a trade caravan leaving in a few days. You can join them. The rest of us will depart in the morning for the mountains." Their destination was Tibet.

They walked to the inn, Sanum strolling silently beside Mitre. Mitre's throat was tight, and he wondered if Sanum felt sad or if monastic discipline had curbed her emotions. Mitre slowed his pace, and they fell behind the others.

"Sanum," Mitre said, "I have taken my own vows to serve Appakke Nakte by living as a monk while carrying out my role as prince."

Sanum faced him. In the moonlight, Mitre saw her tears. "You must marry," she said, wiping her eyes. "You must carry on the royal line of the Kushans."

"I will appoint an heir," Mitre replied. "There is only one who is part of me as my mother was part of my father."

"Perhaps," said Sanum, "but Buddha desires his children to be practical."

"You serve him, and I will also," Mitre affirmed.

Sanum bowed her head. "As you wish," she said. "We must rejoin the others." The group reached the inn together.

AS THE FIRST RAYS OF DAWN STRETCHED OVER THE MUD plaster houses, the travelers stepped outside the inn to meet their guides, who were waiting with a line of small ponies. The travelers shivered and rubbed their arms. Mitre worked hard to contain his sadness from his friends.

Issa stood before him and put his hands on Mitre's shoulders. "Brother," Issa said, "you are right to follow the direction the Almighty places in your heart. Be well. Forgive your father and help him heal. I will see you before I go home."

Sanum mounted a pony. She called to Mitre. As he walked to her side, he realized this could be the last time he would ever see her. "Here," she said, "take these." She pulled off the sandalwood prayer beads that were roped around her arm and pressed them into Mitre's hand. "Pray for me," she said. "I will keep a vigil for you."

At last Lariska came from the inn. She was empty-handed. "Where are your things?" Sanum asked.

"I am going home," Lariska confessed. "I will join the caravan with Mitre."

The color drained from Sanum's face. She held out her arms to Lariska, who quickly hugged her goodbye.

Maitreyajna signaled the guide, who started forward, and all followed. Lariska, overcome with sorrow, hurried back into the inn, but Mitre watched until the figures disappeared over the horizon.

AFTER MANY MONTHS MITRE APPROACHED THE CITY GATES. Sanum's beads were looped around his wrist. He hoped that, wherever she was, she would say a prayer for him now.

"Halt," a tower guard called. "What is your business?"

Mitre looked behind him at the captain of the caravan. The man did not understand Kushan speech. Mitre walked slowly to the gate. Lariska joined him. "Do not tell anyone my true identity," he reminded her. Lariska nodded.

"I am a wandering merchant, born in these lands," Mitre answered in his native tongue. "I want to see your king and offer goods to him and his people. If they are not interested, we will pay for our water and move on."

The guard replied gruffly, "What is your name?"

"Where I travel, I am called Mitre. I have wandered many years, but I remember the words of my people." Mitre boldly stepped forward and loudly sang the folk song from his childhood.

> Ah Shamballa, far away,
> Your sheep are scattered.
> Where are they now, O Ancient Ones?
> Our true leader, Ancient of Days,
> Come, lead us to Shamballa again.

The guard paused, as if he wondered if the singing stranger had drunk too much wine. The sentry disappeared and another took his place. Mitre continued his show.

> Ah Shamballa, far away,
> We long to see your hidden treasures.
> Where is the Sacred Flame kept now?
> Show us once more your secret cave.

The king's advisor, Wenta, peered down from the wall. Strands of white hair blew across his brow. Wenta shielded his eyes from the sun. The scene baffled him: an older Buddhist nun next to a singing man in foreign robes. Behind these two, a caravan of traders idled.

Mitre never paused.

> Ah Shamballa, ever close,
> All I do is close my eyes
> To find my Father and my Mother
> In my own true secret cavern.
> Lead me to Shamballa again.

"Appakke Nakte!" Wenta exclaimed. "Let them in. Send a message to the king that we have visitors. I will take the nun and this man to the great hall. Let the others rest. Provide refreshments for them, and feed and water the livestock."

The gates swung open and the caravan entered, led by Mitre with Lariska alongside.

The streets were busy, though not teeming like the cities of India. Caravans were customary, but the nun and the young man were unusual. Wenta stopped Mitre and looked closely into his face, squinting to see well. Wenta beamed with recognition.

"Say nothing," Mitre warned as he grinned.

Wenta turned to Lariska and studied her face. "Remember me? I'm Lariska," she said. "Your daughter, Sanum, journeys with the others to a mountain monastery."

Wenta warmly greeted Lariska. "Let's go to the great hall," he directed.

Mitre, Lariska, and Wenta walked through the square. A cluster of curious onlookers followed the foreigner, the nun, and the nobleman. By the time Mitre and his escorts stopped at the great hall, they were surrounded by a large throng of people.

Wenta spoke to a guard, who opened the door wide. Mitre froze. He needed time to take in the familiar palace and steady his feelings before meeting his father.

Taktu stood with his men in the middle of the hall. Light from the open door streamed across his graying hair, muslin tunic, and royal blue sash. He scrutinized the three silhouettes at the entrance and noted the entourage of his subjects behind them.

Mitre shivered. His father looked remote and stern. Or, Mitre wondered, was he seeing a reflection of his own pain? "Appakke Nakte," Mitre prayed silently, "melt my father's bitterness and my own. Maitreyajna, Issa, what should I do?"

Mitre dropped to his knees, bowed his head, and crossed his right arm over his chest, placing his fist on his shoulder in homage to the king.

Taktu walked to the entrance, stood before Mitre, and lifted his long-absent son to his feet. The crowd was silent.

The king was stunned with disbelief. He roughly pulled

Mitre's robe from the young man's shoulder. There was the small tattoo with the three tiny flames.

"My son," he said, "you have returned. I greatly erred to burden you with my grief."

"Issa taught me that love endures all things and forgiveness heals all wounds," Mitre replied.

Taktu embraced his son for a long time. At last the king raised Mitre's right arm. Facing the crowd he shouted, "Long live your prince, Vima Kadphises!"

The onlookers roared, waving their hats, scarves, tools—anything they had in their hands—at the bewildering miracle of the prince's return from the dead.

14

MOUNTAIN DISCOVERY

Near Lhasa, Tibet, three years later

AWA PULLED HIS FUR-LINED TUNIC TIGHT. THE LITTLE MAN was bent. Three years in the intense high-altitude weather had aged him. He shivered in the cold morning air as he trudged through snow from his small hut to the entrance of a cave. Bright light streamed in as Awa entered.

A clay oven was built against a side wall. Awa checked the fire. Brass votive lamps burned on a table in front of a small stone statue of Maitreya.

Awa looked beyond the lamps to the back of the short cave, where Issa sat in deep meditation. Under the guidance of a Tibetan master, Issa had continued his contemplative discipline for three years. Awa was happy to bask in the silent peace while working. As he had done routinely for many months since their arrival at the monastery, Awa prepared for Issa a Tibetan meal of barley flour mixed with butter tea. He quietly placed the bowl on the table.

When Awa turned to leave, he was surprised to hear Issa call him. It had been a year since Awa heard Issa speak.

"Master," Awa replied.

Then, he was taken aback and drew in his breath when he saw a brilliant rainbow encircling Issa's head and shoulders. Awa recalled rainbows around some figures in Buddhist paintings they had seen. Mitre, Awa remembered, had been fascinated by them. Awa's mind raced to Mitre's departure. He wondered silently whether Mitre had made it home.

"My friend, you don't need to worry about our brother," Issa said.

The rainbow shimmered—white, yellow, rose, violet, purple, green, and brilliant blue.

"Master, how can I serve you?" Awa asked as he kneeled before Issa.

"Please sit comfortably, Awa," Issa replied. "Don't worship me. What I do is possible for others who strive to become the Buddha.

"You have faithfully cared for me," Issa continued. "You are my first disciple, and you proved your love with courage and service. This spring I will leave the monastery and come down from the mountains. I have met Maitreya."

Awa was astonished. "When, Lord?" he asked. "I have never seen anyone come or go from this cave."

"Last night as you slept," Issa explained, "a wondrous presence appeared to me in my meditation. He had long golden-brown hair. He carried a scepter that glowed with the light of the Almighty. I greeted him with the Hebrew word for father, 'Abba.' I said, '*You* are the teacher, Maitreya, I have searched for all these years. Am I right?'

"Maitreya smiled. 'I am the Coming Buddha. But I may appear in many disguises. You must know that the Coming Buddha is also in you, the poor, the suffering, and the children. Maitreya is everywhere, inspiring compassionate words and wisdom. When you completely become the Christ or the Buddha, you will be everywhere in the consciousness of God. This is breaking the bread of God that is within you and giving it to the many. It is overcoming death. You will show the way of unending life to many, as I do.'

"After these words, Maitreya transformed. He took on the form of an old man. His scepter became a walking stick. I saw the form of Maitreyajna before me. Then he took the form of my meditation teacher. I saw him take the form of many who have guided me in these years of our journey together.

"He said, 'I have been with you from the beginning. You have sought me, and it is well. But I have always been here. And you have met me in the guise of many teachers I have sent you.'

"Tonight he will come again, and he invites you to be present," Issa said.

Awa could hardly fathom that Maitreya had appeared.

There was no fanfare, no build-up. In fact, Awa had practically forgotten about this goal. So much time had gone by that Awa frequently wondered whether Maitreya was real. By now, he assumed that Issa would become a great yogi and no longer be concerned with meeting Maitreya. If Maitreya were to appear, Awa expected a great celebration and clouds of glory. And here Maitreya had been with them all along.

Awa didn't know whether he should be ecstatic or disappointed. He simply accepted the news and believed Issa.

THAT NIGHT AWA KEPT A VIGIL WITH ISSA, RECITING Buddhist mantras. After many hours, Awa noticed a faint glow in the cave. Was there a light beyond what shone from the little butter lamps on the altar? It seemed too early for the dawn.

Then Maitreya appeared. He smiled at Awa, who stood and bowed. Maitreya addressed him. "My student, Awa, year after year you lovingly performed the work given you. Your sacrifices intensified the presence of God in your heart. Tonight the Father enables you to see beyond the physical realm."

A golden aura surrounded Maitreya and filled the room with light. Incredulous, Awa watched and listened as if in another world.

"Abba," Issa began, "what more should I learn before going home?"

"You must be in constant control of the energy of God that flows into you and from you awake or asleep," Maitreya responded. "This is always at the command of a Buddha. You must know, without a doubt, that all things are possible with God. Tonight is your test of oneness with the Father.

"Awa," Maitreya continued, turning to the helper, "it is the Creator's will that you be healed this night if you desire it and if you believe in his power."

"I only want God's will," Awa replied.

"Well said," Maitreya responded. "Issa, hold the uninterrupted vision of Awa whole and complete. Call upon God's infinite power through his presence in your heart. Your concentration must be strong and pure, and you must always ask only for the will of the Father."

Awa felt sleepy and struggled to keep his eyes open. He dreamed of violet light in the form of fire pouring from Issa's heart. Awa felt his back straighten as the pulsation filled him. He watched his withered hand heal. He shook himself awake.

Realizing that his vision was true, Awa impulsively jumped up and extended his hand before him. Incredulous, he alternately spread, flexed, and pinched his fingers. "Praise God!" he shouted as he lifted his arms to heaven.

"You are right," Maitreya said. "God is the healer."

Awa sat down. He rubbed his hand and examined every finger.

Issa remained in prayer, giving thanks. When finished, he said to Maitreya, "Abba, the prophets predict a savior. Some say I am that one. God performed a miracle tonight. Is that what it means to be a savior? What am I meant to do?"

Maitreya pondered before answering. He reasoned that every person finds God's plan through prayer and making wise decisions. Then the divine tapestry for each life naturally unfolds. Was his student Issa different? Should Issa know the future? Would the young man accept it? Was Issa prepared to pay the ultimate price to allow his brothers and sisters more time to balance their karma and realize God within?

Finally, Maitreya replied, "How much do you love? The love of a Christ for his or her brothers and sisters is so great that the blessed one is willing to sacrifice all—even life—to save them and show by action and words the way all must walk to return to God.

"Prophecy is not chiseled in stone and can be changed," Maitreya went on. "You can choose whether or not to take this path. One who would be a Christ or a Buddha is supremely tested—feeling abandoned by our Father—to prove he or she has the mastery to stand alone as a true son or daughter of God. You become one with the Father—and yet retain your identity. A Christ sets the example and goes on to do greater works. So will those who follow in your footsteps.

"It is up to you," Maitreya concluded. "What do you choose, my son?"

IN THE SAME MOUNTAIN RETREAT, SANUM AND ZHU continued their monastic lives. Each spring Zhu gathered herbs, in keeping with his lifelong passion to learn their medicinal effects. Doctors here had much to share.

Sanum wholeheartedly engaged in her practice of prayer, meditation, and writing. She helped provide food for village children and assisted Zhu with his healing work.

They both contemplated which direction to take next.

The news of Maitreya's appearance and Awa's healing spread quickly. Villagers streamed to see the holy man, Issa.

Issa, however, planned his descent from the mountain. It was time to go home. Through his intimate contact with the Father he wore the mantle of the Christ day and night.

15

DOWN FROM
THE MOUNTAIN

Magdala, near the Sea of Galilee, one year later

KING TAKTU'S DAUGHTER, MARY, CELEBRATED HER THIR-
teenth birthday in her mother's land, where Joseph of Arimathea had brought her as an infant. The princess' curly
red hair flowed around her fair and freckled face. Her blue
eyes sparkled with excitement as she looked outside her
aunt and uncle's stone home.

Two visitors arrived today—a man and a woman dressed
in foreign clothes. They sat outside at a table under an olive
tree. Although their expressions looked serious, the woman
often turned to smile warmly at Mary, who stood in the
doorway.

Mary inched closer to her aunt. A warm breeze blew
through the slender silver-green leaves of the olive trees.
Auntie put her arm around the girl's waist.

"Do you remember the story we told you? Your mother
was a queen in the East. She died fighting foreigners who

had invaded her palace. But her handmaid saved you. She wrapped you warmly and handed you to your father, the king, when he came back from his journey. He had been traveling with the older brother you haven't seen since you were an infant.

"Your father was heartbroken when your mother died, and he had no one to raise you. So he sent you to us."

Yes, Mary knew the story well, though she never spoke of it—the mother who was gone like a vapor and the father who had rejected her. It was a gnawing ache that had not diminished in thirteen years.

"These are your father's representatives who have come to speak with you. They have traveled far and must be tired from their journey."

Mary clung tighter to Auntie, the only mother she knew. The visitors had nice faces, but they were strangers. The idea of another father and brother was a hazy and not-too-pleasant concept.

Nevertheless, Mary curiously observed the guests. The man wore a tuniclike coat and trousers. The woman wore a long dress and felt cap. Mary was surprised when they stood and bowed to her. The girl didn't know how to respond. She stiffly bowed to them in return. The adults laughed.

"I am Vitah and this is my wife, Arya," the man said. "We are servants of King Taktu and tutor young members of the Order of Melchizedek in religious training and the arts of war. Your father sent us to offer you training and invite you, as our princess, to visit your true home. Perhaps you will like it there." Vitah smiled.

Mary frowned.

"The king asked us to settle here in your town," Vitah went on. "I think you will enjoy learning the ways of the Order."

"And this," Arya added, "is for you." She handed Mary a small, exquisitely carved cedar box.

Mary ran her fingers over the intricate design of interlaced angles and triangles. She slowly opened the box, and her face lit up when she saw the beautiful gold Signet. A gold chain glittered behind the medallion.

"It belongs to your father," Arya said. "Here, let me put it on you." She unlocked the chain and hooked it around Mary's neck and under her long hair.

"The members of the Order of Melchizedek know you by this medal," Vitah said. "Never betray the trust." He placed his hand upon Mary's head and blessed her.

Nazareth, the same time

MARY, THE MOTHER OF JESUS, WAS ABSORBED IN THOUGHT as she looked out the window of the home her son once shared with his family. There was not a day—in fact, there was hardly an hour—when she did not breathe a prayer for the safe return of her sojourning child.

Her next son, James, was not a worry. He was already married and his wife was expecting a child soon. His new house adjoined Mary's, making one large home. Mary and her daughter, Miriam, had lived in James' home since the death of Mary's husband, Joseph.

Miriam was a lovely young woman in her prime years for marriage. Mary had sent a message to her cousin Elisabeth inquiring about her son, John, as he might be a suitable prospect for Miriam's husband. Their families were already bonded by prophecies surrounding their offspring.

"Strange," Mary mused, "how the angels carry our thoughts to others. I no sooner sent my message than Miriam burst into the house with news of John's holy work."

Mary recalled the scene. A small prayer group had gathered, as they did many evenings, in her home. Mary wondered why Miriam was late, when the young woman, out of breath from running, hurried in the door.

Miriam took the shawl from her shoulders and hung it over a peg. Turning to the group, she said excitedly, "Have you heard of one of our people named John? He preaches that we should repent our sins. Hundreds go to hear him. Then he cleanses them in the river to make them new. It's wonderful. I saw him this afternoon."

"Is this the son of Elisabeth?" Mary asked. Miriam

nodded. Mary added, "He and Jesus spent many hours to-gether. It's been years since I've seen him. What does he say? Is it truth?"

"Surely," Miriam answered animatedly. The fire gleaming out of the lamp cast a glow over the young woman's face and red cheeks. The guests talked excitedly. Some of them knew of John.

"He challenged the priests and warned them of God's anger," Miriam continued. "He said the axe would cut trees that did not give good fruit. People asked him what to do. John told them to repent of their sins and to be kind to one another. He said if they had two coats, give one to the poor, and if they had meat, to do the same."

One of Mary's guests, a grandmother, said, "Some people think he is the Messiah."

"No," Miriam answered. "John says that he baptizes men and women with water, but that one who is greater will baptize them with fire and the Holy Spirit."

"Who comes to hear him?" Mary asked.

"Everyone," Miriam replied. "People love him. Even soldiers listen."

"I'll go with you tomorrow," Mary said. "We'll invite him to our home for supper. But be careful, Miriam. John's words may be dangerous in the eyes of the governor. We should keep John in our prayers."

A grandfather asked, "What news do you have of Jesus?

He has been gone many years now."

Mary smiled. She went to an alcove in the wall near the lamp and picked up the yellow cloth package that Joseph of Arimathea delivered years ago. "I have this," she replied.

Mary carefully unfolded the yellow cloth until it covered her lap. She gently turned the flattened palm leaves over one at a time, resting them on her knees as she read. She recounted her son's travels in the East, until she came to the end and read, "Greet all who serve my Father. Grace be with you."

Mary rewrapped the letter. She looked troubled. The grandmother stood and put her hand on Mary's shoulder. "Jesus will return," she told Mary comfortingly.

Mary nodded weakly. "Yes," she agreed. "I had an unusual dream a few nights ago."

"Can you tell us?" the woman asked.

"A fine man appeared," Mary recounted. "He looked the same age as Jesus. The man had long golden-brown hair. I sensed he was Jesus' teacher. Jesus wrote that he was looking for Maitreya. I guessed this was Maitreya."

"What did he say?" Miriam asked.

"He said, 'Do not be afraid. Your son returns.'" Mary paused.

"That's a wonderful dream," the grandfather exclaimed. "Jesus is coming home."

Miriam noticed her mother remained troubled. She sat beside Mary and took her hand. "Our group will pray tonight for Jesus and his safe return."

All agreed and bowed their heads.

Mary was grateful for the prayers. She could not share with anyone the end of her dream. In it she cried as she embraced her son's limp and bloody body, which lay on the ground next to a heavy timber cross.

Kashmir, the same time

THE JOURNEY FROM LHASA WAS LONG AND DIFFICULT. A guide had escorted Issa, Sanum, Zhu, and Awa through the mountains to Ladakh, where they visited a small monastery. Issa taught in the dusty hall where monks and nuns sat on mats and absorbed his words about Buddha and Maitreya.

Sanum felt at home with the other nuns, more than she ever recalled in these many years of travel. It was time for her choice. She could go back to Kapisa and everyone she loved— including Mitre—or sacrifice her desires in order to answer a calling she felt in her heart. After nights of deep prayer and painful mental wrestling, she reluctantly decided to remain and write down the story of Issa and Maitreya. "I'll pray for all of you," she said. "This is a good place for meditation and writing. I know I'm meant to stay." In a quaking voice she added, "But you must go and show people the way to Shamballa in their hearts."

"You are a daughter of the Most High," Issa replied, "and you have sacrificed everything to be one with the Father."

"In my small way, I hope my prayers and chronicles help your mission. Tell my parents and Mitre that I am well and happy," she answered. "Here, I prepared letters for them." Sanum handed Issa a long, cloth-wrapped package that fit in his leather pouch. "Be well, my friends. Go quickly. I won't be able to bear it if you leave slowly. My bravery will last only a few moments more."

Issa, Awa, and Zhu mounted ponies and followed their guide through the town, where villagers lined the road to send them off. Bells jingled around the ponies' necks. After leaving the crowd, the only other sounds were plodding hooves and the wind in the canyons.

After many days of travel, they reached a lower town of Kashmir and rested at an inn for several weeks before continuing their journey through India. Here, as everywhere else they went, villagers came to listen to Issa.

One balmy afternoon, Issa and Awa strolled together. Fruit trees blossomed and tall pines loomed, foreshadowing the mountains. Streams rushed with white water.

"Awa," Issa said, "a new role is coming to you, if you are willing."

Awa looked puzzled, but nodded his eagerness to serve.

Issa put his hand on Awa's shoulder. "Are you willing to remain behind as we continue without you?"

Awa's heart sank. He bowed low and asked, "Master, what have I done?"

Issa replied, "I grew up under your care. You have great courage and love for me and my Father. But I need your service here—to prepare for my return."

Awa looked bewildered.

"Come," Issa said, "let's go back into the village." They walked into town. "Will you prepare a home here for me? I will come back after several years. You can teach here. It's a beautiful place for meditation."

Awa considered life without his master. It was impossible. Awa had never been alone, a free man with two hands, no barriers, no caste identity, no shackles of any kind, not even a monkey—only himself. The prospect was frightening and paralyzing.

Issa instantly understood Awa's swirling emotions and their cause. "Awa," he said, "you are a son of God. Now it is your time to teach. And, I ask you to pray for me and my Father's work.

"You decide," Issa continued. "Tomorrow, Zhu and I will leave with the guide and travel down the Indus River and on to King Taktu's palace. You can continue with us if you choose. Our Father will tell you in your heart."

The next day, Awa, Zhu, and Issa ate breakfast together in silence. Issa noticed there were no bundles next to Awa's pony, which was tied outside with the others. He also noticed deep rings under Awa's red eyes, as if he had not slept. "Brother," Issa said, "I love you with all my heart."

"I will make all ready for you, Master," Awa said in a cracking voice. "And you, too, Master Zhu. You must hurry back to this place where a home will be waiting for you. You must be careful."

They walked outside to the waiting ponies. "You will be proud," Awa said through tears. Issa wiped his own eyes.

Zhu embraced Awa and gave him a small stone container, no wider than a large coin. "Very special," Zhu explained. "I learned this mixture in the mountains where I gathered the herbs myself. Mix it in a cup with water. After a few sips, you will sleep. You look tired, my friend. You deserve a good rest."

Awa laughed. Through the years, he had grown to understand the subtle and loving humor of his Eastern friend.

Issa, Zhu, and the guide started down the road. Awa cried loudly, waving and bowing as they disappeared from view.

Kapisa, some months later

PRINCE VIMA KADPHISES STOOD IMPATIENTLY IN THE WATCH-tower of his father's palace. He had scanned the horizon every day since his father's friend, Caspar, had arrived a month ago.

"It is in the stars," Caspar had said over dinner with Vima and Taktu. "Jesus, or Issa, as you call him, will come soon. That's why I am here. Do you think it is to see you, you old goat?" Caspar chided Taktu.

"I will personally escort him through my lands," Caspar continued, "and make sure he arrives back home. It's time for him to begin his work, don't you think?" Caspar shook his head and thought of the state of affairs in kingdoms beyond his land. Most lived in subjugation to the Romans, poverty was rampant, and religion was tolerated as long as it did not interfere with the deified Roman emperors.

"I'll go with you," Vima interjected.

"If you ask me," Caspar said, "your Appakke Nakte has other plans for you. You are needed here, son. You must start a family."

"I choose to live a monk's life in this palace. I learned from Issa and Maitreyajna that I can live in the world but not be of the world."

"You have learned a great deal since I last saw you," remarked Caspar, laughing. "And do you think I staged your death so many years ago only to have my friend's royal bloodline end with you?"

"My sister can marry and continue the bloodline," Vima responded.

"Yes," Caspar agreed. "I'm sure she will have her role to play."

Vima directed the conversation away from his future. "Issa can carry out his mission here. Our land is open to him. We welcome a prophet and messiah."

Caspar became serious. "It's true. This is a great land, and someday you will make it even greater. But the prophets say that Jesus must begin his mission with his own people, and then his example will spread to the world. He must go home, though I fear his work will not be easy."

Taktu interrupted. "Issa will do exactly as his Father tells him, and you, my son, will also know clearly what you are to do by the direction Appakke Nakte places in your heart."

Vima nodded. He knew from experience there were no truer words.

A hot wind blew across Vima's face as he stood in the watchtower along the city wall. For a long time his eyes fixed on a small cloud of dust at the horizon. Caravans came along the road almost every week. But this cloud was too small to be a caravan. No, the livestock looked more like horses being led. Perhaps they were wandering merchants or tradesmen. As they came closer, the horses looked too small. "Ponies," Vima thought, "unusual for this land."

The two approaching strangers sometimes walked in single file, sometimes side by side. They were alone. As they drew closer, Vima saw that no caravan followed in the distance. The sun behind them made it difficult to see details. "What are the colors they are wearing? Saffron? Burgundy?

Brown? What do the people look like?" Vima strained to get a better view.

At last Vima made out white robes blowing in the breeze, and then he knew.

"Issaaa!" he shouted and waved his arms. The prince charged down the steps, threw open the gates, and ran along the road.

"Zhuuu! Issaaa!" he shouted as he rushed to greet them. The friends embraced.

THAT EVENING TAKTU, CASPAR, WENTA, VIMA, ZHU, AND Issa sat together for a simple meal. The occasion of their reunion was joyous, but they were not jovial. They spoke quietly and comfortably. The younger men shared with their elders the humorous and poignant experiences of their travel together.

All perceived changes in one another. Issa's demeanor was peaceful and reflective, yet exuded heightened awareness of his Father and the needs of the Father's children.

Much of the bitterness had left Taktu. He looked contented.

Zhu was outgoing and humorous. His words were measured and wise.

Vima no longer carried the anger of his youth. He was self-assured. "Thank you for bringing the letters from Sanum," he said to Issa.

Wenta, Sanum's father, nodded and spoke to Issa. "She is writing your stories and feels her place is at the monastery in Ladakh. I grieve that her mother and these old eyes of mine may never see her in this life."

"You will see her again," Issa prophesied. "It is the Father's desire to grant this for your sacrifice. Take heart. Your work for the Order bears much fruit."

Vima noted Issa's implication that Sanum could possibly return, but he dared not entertain that expectation. His determination was set on living his royal life with the Kushans as a monk.

"What are your plans?" Vima asked Zhu and Issa.

"I'm here to keep you healthy," Zhu laughed, "and to spread the teachings of Buddha," he continued. "Let me tell you the story of an amazing healing." Without exaggeration, Zhu recounted everything that Awa had told him about the night with Maitreya when Issa had called for the healing of Awa's hand.

"From this I have learned," Zhu concluded, "that God is the healer. Everything I do with herbs and prayers may assist him in some small way to comfort his children in pain, but it does not compare to a Son who has union with him. Issa's example teaches us that we must all seek this union and do the works of the Father as he does.

"So, I am here, if you will have me, to be the court physician and serve you until it is the will of God for me to complete a different task for the Order."

Pleased, Taktu nodded in agreement. Vima, sitting at Zhu's side, slapped his old friend on the back and ladled more food onto Zhu's plate. "Enough!" Zhu protested, laughing again.

"And you, Issa?" Vima inquired, hoping for a response similar to Zhu's to dispel the predictions of Caspar.

"I must go home," Issa said plainly, yet everyone sensed an ominous importance behind those words. They didn't know why.

Issa explained. "I am the way. Those of my land must see me and be with me day by day, so I can demonstrate the truth that the Father dwells in me and wants to live in them also. I must teach them that death is not real."

No one spoke. They all wondered how this was to be accomplished. It was a daunting mission, to say the least, and dangerous. All remained silent.

Finally, Vima spoke softly. "We need you here to prove this. There is much grief and pain among the Kushans. We lost our home generations ago and long for our ancient sacred place, Shamballa."

"But here," Issa said, "you live close to Buddha and Krishna. These great teachers have come. They have also shown the way and the truth. Be like them and comfort the Kushan people."

Vima agreed that he must help fulfill the words of

Issa for the Kushans. It was his love of Issa that made him reluctant to let the man go. There was nothing he could do but once again face the pain of separation—and this time rise above it.

Caspar interjected, "My men are here to escort you safely back."

"They may come as my followers," Issa replied, "but not as my guards. Our Father travels with us day and night."

FOR SEVERAL DAYS ISSA STAYED WITH THE KUSHANS AND taught. Finally the morning arrived for his departure.

As usual, a crowd gathered to walk for a distance with their teacher and his companions. Taktu embraced Issa and said goodbye. Wenta and Zhu knelt and asked for blessings. Issa touched their heads and helped the old man up. Then Issa looked at the tower by the Kapisa gate. Once again Vima stood in that high spot—this time so he would be able to see Issa all the way to the horizon.

As they gazed at one another in silent farewell, Vima touched Sanum's prayer beads, which he still wore wrapped around his arm. He took them off and started repeating prayers for Issa as his thumb and index finger rolled over the beads. Issa waved goodbye as his throat burned with emotion and his eyes filled. Vima stopped his prayer, wiped his eyes, waved his arm overhead, and shouted, "Long live

Issa!" The crowd repeated his salutation several times as Issa turned to go.

"May all life be blessed," Vima said softly and then continued his prayers.

"These books say your Jesus was here."

Tibetan Buddhist Librarian, Himis Monastery, Ladakh, 1939

CAST OF CHARACTERS

(Alphabetical Order, Main Characters)

Awa Servant of Joseph of Arimathea. One of his hands was rendered useless by Indian authorities as punishment for listening to the Vedas. Joseph of Arimathea sent Awa traveling with Jesus.

Bashir See *Panum Sri Bashir.*

Caspar A king in the area of Persia and one of the Three Wise Men, who had traveled to visit the Holy Family at the birth of Jesus. A close friend of King Taktu, Caspar comes to the rescue of the king during an attack by the Huns.

Hanuman The pet monkey owned by Awa.

Issa In the story, the name given to Jesus to disguise his identity while traveling in India and the Himalayas. The name for Jesus used in Buddhist scriptures from Ladakh.

Jesus Also called Issa in the East and in Buddhist scriptures.

Joseph of Arimathea Mentioned in the Gospels, Joseph of Arimathea is thought to be a trader and wealthy relative of Jesus. He persuaded Pontius Pilate to allow him to take the crucified body of Jesus and lay it in his own personal tomb. Legends tell of Joseph of Arimathea in Glastonbury and of taking the boy Jesus to study there.

Joseph of Nazareth Husband of Mary. Protector of Mary and Jesus.

King Vima Taktu Taktu. King Taktu. Historical king in the lineage of the Kushan empire. Father of Vima Kadphises (Vima), who travels as Mitre with Issa in the story.

Lahore Young teenage girl in India who is kidnapped by Bashir. Her family is in the trade of weaving silk rugs. Later, she follows Issa.

Lariska Early in the story, Lariska is a nursemaid to Queen Sarah, who is the wife of King Taktu. Lariska is later a matronly chaperone to the young travelers—Issa, Zhu, Mitre, and Sanum—who accompany Maitreyajna. Awa also travels with the group.

Maitreya A Bodhisattva, often referred to as the Coming Buddha, representing the potential Buddha-nature in humankind.

Maitreyajna Unchanging, ageless shepherd who delivers important messages to King Taktu and other colleagues in the Order of Melchizedek. He later leads Issa, Mitre, Zhu, Sanum, Lariska, and Awa on the search for Maitreya.

Mary Name given to the infant daughter of King Taktu and the deceased Queen Sarah. The infant is taken by Joseph of Arimathea to her relatives in Magdala.

Mary Mother of Jesus. Jesus names Taktu's infant daughter after her.

Mitre Name given to Prince Vima Kadphises (Vima) to disguise his identity in India and the Himalayas.

Panum Sri Bashir Wealthy warlord and landowner who attempts to enslave a teenage girl, Lahore, and later challenges Issa.

Prince Vima Kadphises Historical prince and later king in the lineage of the Kushans. In the beginning of the story, he is called yekte ("little") Vima. After his tenth birthday he is called Vima. During his travels in India and the East, his name is changed to Mitre to disguise his identity.

Queen Sarah Wife of King Taktu. Mother of Vima.

Sanum Friend and peer of the prince, Vima. She is the daughter of King Taktu's advisor, Wenta.

Sarah See *Queen Sarah.*

Taktu See *King Vima Taktu.*

Vali Hindu head priest in Mathura. Bashir's friend.

Vima See *Prince Vima Kadphises.*

Wenta Chief advisor to King Taktu and head priest for the Kushans. Father of Sanum, who travels with Issa, Mitre, Zhu, and the others in India and the East.

Zhu Surname for two characters, but for most of the book it refers to Zhu Ying, the son of Zhu Li. The father, Zhu Li, is a medical practitioner and helper to King Taktu. The son, Zhu Ying (Zhu), is a medical practitioner and companion to the king's son, Vima.

THE ORDER OF MELCHIZEDEK

The Order of Melchizedek is mentioned in the Old and New Testaments of the Bible. The passages reproduced here are taken from the King James Version.

And Melchizedek king of Salem brought forth bread and wine: and he was the priest of the most high God. And he blessed him and said, Blessed be Abram of the most high God, possessor of heaven and earth: and blessed be the most high God, which hath delivered thine enemies into thy hand. And he gave him tithes of all.

Genesis 14:18–20

Whither the forerunner is for us entered, even Jesus, made an high priest for ever after the order of Melchisedec.

For this Melchisedec, king of Salem, priest of the most high God, who met Abraham returning from the slaughter of the kings, and blessed him; to whom also Abraham gave a tenth part of all; first being by interpretation King of righteousness, and after that also King of Salem, which is, King of peace; without father, without mother, without descent, having neither beginning of days, nor end of life; but made like unto the Son of God; abideth a priest continually.

Hebrews 6:20; 7:1–3

ACKNOWLEDGMENTS

This novel would not be possible without the landmark work of author, teacher, and lecturer Elizabeth Clare Prophet in her publication *The Lost Years of Jesus*. Mrs. Prophet sparked my quest to strive to understand and internalize Jesus' timeless message that permeates the mystical paths of the world religions. For this I am deeply grateful.

My special thanks go to my collaborator, Fred Peck, whose research into the lost years of Jesus, the history of the Kushans, and the Tokharian language provided the background material and story line for this book.

Fred and I would like to thank the many authors and scholars at Harvard University, the University of Washington, the University of Idaho, the University of Pennsylvania, the University of British Columbia, and many others, who provided valuable insights and inspiration. A special thanks to Daniel Entin of the Nicholas Roerich Museum in New York City.

Many friends and colleagues have assisted with comments and editing of the manuscript. My gratitude goes to each and every one for your prayers, your time, your belief in this project, and for cheering me on. My special thanks to Kate Gordon, JoAnn Jensen, Annice Booth, and Norman Millman—your reviews and support were essential.

The team of Rosemary Dickie, Orion and Helen Beaufort, Joseph Angeles, and others of their friends—along with Ken Wilson—contributed vital feedback. Your perceptions helped provide the link to the main character of the ages, Jesus.

For their invaluable assistance, I wish to thank Robert Fulton, Brooke Foster, and Karen Gordon for their patient editing work; Lynn Wilbert for her beautiful book design; and Meira Dor and Thom Schumacher for their support and marketing expertise.

I am grateful to my friends in Tibet, especially Bangdu Rinpoche, Nyima Choedron, and Ani, who exemplified the compassion of the masters of the East.

Last, but not least, I am deeply grateful to my husband, Stephen, whose love and dedication to our marriage and to my professional and spiritual growth are a constant source of inspiration for which I am very blessed.

READER'S SECTION

Reflection and Dialogue

Dear Friends,

It is my sincere hope that you enjoyed this story about Jesus and what it may have been like for him as a youth—especially if he traveled to India as a number of scholars and investigators believe. It has been thrilling for me to spend quiet time contemplating the portions of his childhood and young adulthood that are missing from the Bible yet survive in legends and in our imaginations.

I would like nothing better than to share this experience with you. For this reason, I offer here a few questions for your private meditation, your further reading, or for discussion with a group of friends.

If you're gathering with friends and talking about the book, have a good time. I wish I could be physically with you! But you're welcome to e-mail your questions or comments to LoisDrake@SnowMountainPress.com. If you have a speakerphone, I'd also be happy to spend a few minutes with your group.

Here we go! Have a great adventure.

1. Why did you decide to read *Issa: The Greatest Story Never Told?* What is the message you received from it? Does that message affect you personally? How?

2. What do you think Jesus would have been like if you had met him during these years? Did any of the scenes from his teen or early adult years hold special meaning for you? If yes, what was special?

3. Many of the characters reflect emotions we can all identify with. Which character was your favorite? Why? Do any of the characters remind you of yourself or someone you know?

4. On page 2 we read, "... a six-pointed star, with a three-part flame at its center. The Signet." The Signet first appears in chapter one and then throughout the book. What does it symbolize for you?

5. One of the main ideas in the story is that Jesus had a teacher to guide him in his mission and development. How do you feel about this concept? What implications does it have?

6. I wanted to show the struggle the characters faced in trying to determine God's will. What were some scenes where you thought characters did *not* make the best choices? How do you personally figure out the next best step in your life?

7. In the story, as Jesus traveled by ship to India, I wrote, "Whatever the sons and daughters of the Creator did to

advance light and understanding among men and women was often opposed by forces of darkness."

What do you think of this theory? If you have seen this in your life or the lives of others, can you give some examples? What do you believe is the antidote?

8. The girl Sanum wanted to go on the journey with Maitrey-ajna. Why do you think she wanted to do this? Have you ever dropped everything to follow a path you felt was right even though it was difficult? What was the result?

9. When Jesus told the story of the Pharaoh and the slaves, the audience was shocked and said, "They are slaves because of their karma."

What are your thoughts about karma and reincarnation and the idea of creating positive or negative karma? Do you think Jesus believed in karma and reincarnation?

I know there are many more questions that can be discussed and pondered. May all of them draw us closer to tolerance, patience, understanding, forgiveness, and love for one another and the divinity placed within our hearts.

Sincerely,
Lois Drake

NOTES

NOTES

HISTORICAL PERSPECTIVE
ON THE
KUSHAN EMPIRE

When I first reviewed the archeological findings about the Kushan civilization, I was intrigued by the possibility of an interconnection between this people and Jesus during his "lost years," ages 13 to 29, unrecorded in the Bible.

The Kushan information, combined with stories of Jesus in India and Nepal—from mysterious Buddhist records and legends—gave me a vehicle for my fictional account of a young boy who would someday become a spiritual king.

If a teenaged Jesus had traveled east as postulated in several works citing the Buddhist documents and regional folklore, he would have encountered the influence and possibly even the key players of the Kushan kingdom. The Kushans established a large empire throughout ancient Bactria and portions of modern China, Afghanistan, Iran, Pakistan, and India. Their kingdom flourished well into the third century.

Who were the Kushans and where did they come from?

The mystery begins in the northwestern desert of China, in the sands of the Tarim Basin along an ancient silk route. There, in the early 1900s, explorers and archeologists began to unearth mummified bodies, many of them perfectly preserved, with their clothing intact, as a result of the dry desert conditions. The oldest mummies are about 4,000 years old.

Western scholars have long known of their existence, but the mummies became more widely researched and discussed beginning in the 1980s and '90s. Scholars sometimes refer to them collectively as the mummies of Ürümchi, named for the town in China's Uyghur Autonomous Region in which they are housed.

The mummified bodies raise interesting questions. These people had neither Chinese nor Mongolian characteristics. The hair of the mummies is light colored—blonde to light brown or shades of red. Their stature is tall. Their noses are high bridged. The patterns of their woven wool fabrics are similar to ancient Celtic or European patterns.*

From ancient Chinese accounts, we know that a nomadic people called the Yueh-chih settled in the Tarim Basin and coexisted peacefully with the Chinese prior to the time of Jesus' birth. Eventually one of their kings, Kajula Kadphises, succeeded in rising to power and uniting them. They became known as the Kushan people.

Although the Yueh-chih/Kushans coexisted peacefully with the Chinese, they were at war with the ancestors of the central Asian Huns. The first attacks of the Huns drove them from the Tarim Basin and its surrounding mountains, and they subsequently migrated into the area of Afghanistan and northern India.

*See Elizabeth Wayland Barber, The Mummies of Ürümchi (New York: W. W. Norton & Company, 1999).

We find evidence of their empire in the art, coins, gold decorations, statues, and stone tablet work of the region. The Kushan influence extended east to Iran and then further south into Pakistan and India. In the second century, a Kushan ruler, Kanishka, assembled a Buddhist council that was instrumental in the spread of the Mahayana school of Buddhism. Yet he and previous Kushan kings fostered religious tolerance, which enabled Hinduism and a panoply of religions to flourish in the area side by side.

Investigators theorize that some of the people traveled back to the Tarim Basin, where scholars have found Buddhist texts written in the now-extinct Tokharian language. A number of authorities believe Tokharian, unknown until the beginning of the twentieth century, may have been the language of the Yueh-chi/Kushans.

As I contemplated these facts, the historical setting of my story evolved. I chose to juxtapose the challenges of the worldly kingdom of the Kushan royalty with the wisdom of the East and the trials of the young Jesus in an unfamiliar land.

The ancient people provided material to portray the preparation of two future kings—one to inherit an earthly realm and one who would become known as the Savior.

Lois Drake

FOR FURTHER READING

If you would like to learn more about the "lost years" of Jesus or the Kushan civilization, the following sources are recommended:

The Lost Years of Jesus: Documentary Evidence of Jesus' 17-Year Journey to the East, by Elizabeth Clare Prophet (Summit University Press, 1987).

Mrs. Prophet presents the accounts of four eyewitnesses who investigated or were shown the Buddhist manuscripts chronicling Saint Issa's (Jesus') life and message in the East. She also publishes in the book three variant translations of these remarkable texts.

The Mummies of Ürümchi, by Elizabeth Wayland Barber (W. W. Norton & Company, 1999).

Ms. Barber recounts the discovery of ancient mummies in a remote area of central Asia and the subsequent findings and details about the lives, migration and evolution of the people who eventually became known as the Kushans.

www.kushan.org   This Web site contains a wealth of information, including articles on the history of the Kushans, their art and coinage. It is updated with reports from academic journals and contains reviews of books and articles for further study about the Kushan Empire.

The Lost Years of Jesus
Documentary Evidence
of Jesus' 17-Year Journey to the East
by Elizabeth Clare Prophet

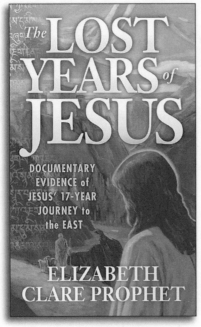

ISBN: 978-0-916766-87-0
pocketbook $9.95

Ancient texts reveal that Jesus spent 17 years in the Orient. They say that from age thirteen to age twenty-nine Jesus traveled to India, Nepal, Ladakh, and Tibet as both student and teacher.

For the first time Elizabeth Clare Prophet brings together the testimony of four eyewitnesses—and three variant translations—of these remarkable documents.

She tells the intriguing story of how Russian journalist Nicolas Notovitch discovered the manuscripts in a monastery in Ladakh in 1887. Critics "proved" they did not exist—and then three distinguished scholars and educators rediscovered them in the 20th century.

Now you can read for yourself what Jesus said and did prior to his Palestinian mission.

Illustrated with maps, drawings and 79 photos.

Lost Teachings of Jesus:
Missing Texts • Karma and Reincarnation
by Elizabeth Clare Prophet

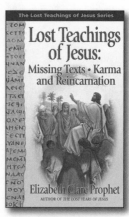

Some accounts report Jesus teaching for hours, yet do not record what the Master said. Mark and Elizabeth Prophet show that many of Jesus' original teachings were lost, tampered with or suppressed.

In *Lost Teachings of Jesus: Missing Texts • Karma and Reincarnation* the Prophets fill in the gaps with a bold reconstruction of the essence of Jesus' message and answer questions that have puzzled readers of the Bible for centuries.

ISBN: 978-0-916766-90-0
pocketbook $7.99

Their fresh approach, combined with penetrating research and anecdotes, makes this book compelling reading.

Mary Magdalene and the Divine Feminine
Jesus' Lost Teachings on Woman
by Elizabeth Clare Prophet with Annice Booth

What was Jesus' relationship with Mary Magdalene? Why was Jesus' message on reverence for Woman and on the inner potential of both man and woman suppressed? Is God only male? Does celibacy work for priests? Ancient texts reveal the answers.

ISBN: 978-1-932890-06-8
softbound $15.95

Includes 55 illustrations, two maps and discussion questions.

FOR MORE INFORMATION

Snow Mountain Press and Summit University Press books are available at fine bookstores worldwide and online at your favorite booksellers and at www.SummitUniversityPress.com.

For a free catalog of Summit University Press books and products or for information about interviews and book signings by Lois Drake, please contact:

Summit University Press
63 Summit Way, Gardiner, MT 59030 USA

Tel: 1-800-245-5445 or 406-848-9500
Fax: 1-800-221-8307 or 406-848-9555

E-mail: info@SummitUniversityPress.com

www.ISSA-TheGreatestStoryNeverTold.com

SNOW MOUNTAIN ▲ PRESS™
An imprint of Summit University Press